How Everyone on the

Autism Spectrum,

Young and Old, can...

become RESILIENT,
be more OPTIMISTIC,
enjoy HUMOR,
be KIND, and
increase SELF-EFFICACY

A Positive Psychology Approach

June Groden,
Ayelet Kantor,
Cooper R. Woodard,
and Lewis P. Lipsitt

Foreword by V. Mark Durand, Ph.D.

Jessica Kingsley *Publishers*
London and Philadelphia

First published in 2011
by Jessica Kingsley Publishers
116 Pentonville Road
London N1 9JB, UK
and
400 Market Street, Suite 400
Philadelphia, PA 19106, USA

www.jkp.com

Copyright © June Groden, Ayelet Kantor, Cooper R. Woodard, and Lewis P. Lipsitt 2011
Foreword copyright © V. Mark Durand

Library of Congress Cataloging in Publication Data
A CIP catalog record for this book is available from the Library of Congress

British Library Cataloguing in Publication Data
A CIP catalogue record for this book is available from the British Library

ISBN 978 1 84905 853 7

Printed and bound in the United States

*To the staff at the Groden Network who work tirelessly
to enhance the lives of the children and adults we support*

ACKNOWLEDGMENTS

This volume is the product of four years of collaboration by the clinical licensed psychologists and supervisory staff at the Groden Center in Providence, Rhode Island. The Groden Center is a treatment and educational program supporting children and adults with autism and other pervasive developmental disabilities. At our training and clinical meetings, we have devoted two hours a month to the study of positive psychology. Cooper R. Woodard, Ph.D., provided a basic orientation to the field of positive psychology at the initial meetings. In addition, we divided into five groups for more intensive study of the five areas that were chosen for this book: optimism, humor, self-efficacy, kindness, and resilience. Contributors listed on page 14 did the research for the narratives, and developed and field tested the activities. Persons listed as writers wrote the narratives. The project coordinator, Ayelet Kantor, Ph.D., was responsible for providing a cohesive effort for this undertaking. She garnered material from the committees and from her own extensive research, and was responsible for the majority of the writing. We appreciate all her efforts as well as all of the professionals who contributed. Finally, our administrative assistant, Linda Ollari, has been of tremendous help in all the logistical aspects of pulling the book together. We thank you.

June Groden

CONTENTS

Foreword

> We hold these truths to be self-evident, that all men are created equal,
> that they are endowed by their Creator with certain unalienable Rights,
> that among these are Life, Liberty and the pursuit of Happiness. (The
> Declaration of Independence)

I remember the day as if it were yesterday. My wife was in labor for almost 24 hours and things were not progressing. After several requests, I finally made it clear to the obstetrician that a cesarean section was called for and he finally agreed. Not long after that conversation my wife was no longer in agony and my son entered the world. Little during that time is or was very clear – just a flurry of activity by doctors and nurses. Ten fingers and toes, and so on. Finally, like an angel, a nurse wrapped up my newborn son and led us to a small and quiet room where I could hold him and let it all sink in. This was it. All of the discussions, planning, worries, and anticipation were over. Here he was in my arms.

As I held this little wonder against me a song by Roy Orbison drifted through my mind – 'Anything You Want (You Got It).' Of all of the discussions about what he might grow up to be, where he might go to school, and who he might love, the only thing I could think of at that point was 'Would he be happy?' My only wish and prayer for him was to lead a happy life. President or professor? Actor or accountant? Stanford or state university? It didn't matter as long as he was happy.

This is the wish of all parents – that their child leads a happy and fulfilled life. This seemingly small hope, however, is often elusive. Life has a way of intervening and getting in the way of happiness for all of us. People become ill, they have money problems or relationship problems.

There are disappointments and tragedies. We do know that people differ in their level of happiness, independent of what they face in life. But, we also are learning that our level of happiness (sometimes called 'subjective well-being') can be increased through practicing certain things such as looking at problems in a more optimistic way, being grateful for what you do have ('counting your blessings'), and being more mindful about what is going on around us (e.g., noticing that your daughter likes watching bugs).

This longing for happiness for your child is ubiquitous among parents of children with autism spectrum disorders (ASD). Whether the effects of ASD are viewed as a curse or a blessing, these families all wish for their child to be comfortable, worry-free and to have times when the world seems like a wonderful place to live. They often express a desire that their child has friends and meaningful social relationships. For over three decades, June and Gerry Groden and their colleagues at the internationally recognized Groden Center have had a deep understanding of this need on the part of parents. While the field of ASD focused on reducing problem behaviors and teaching skills, they extended this work to helping people with ASD learn to relax in the face of adverse situations (e.g., loud noises, too many people around) and to help them reduce their stress. This focus on the quality of life in addition to academic and social skills training puts them at the forefront of efforts to improve happiness or subjective well-being among people with ASD.

In this new book, June Groden and many of the professionals and staff at the Groden Center provide us with a groundbreaking blueprint for how to help foster and nurture characteristics such as optimism, humor, self-efficacy, kindness, and resilience among people across the lifespan who have ASD. They begin by introducing readers to the growing field of positive psychology, a recent expansion of historic efforts to understand and help people become happier. They then provide a way to assess positive character traits using a scale developed at the Groden Center (Assessment Scale for Positive Character Traits – Developmental Disabilities; ASPeCT-DD). This scale will be helpful to parents, teachers, and staff to determine a person's current level of functioning in areas such as the ability to show caring for others, the ability to understand humor, and to be persistent when faced with difficulties. It will also prove useful to see if changes occur in these areas once the techniques described throughout the book are employed.

It is important to point out that this scale and the other tools provided in the book are consistent with the authors' desire to be evidence-based with their work. Each of the very helpful exercises they provide has been field tested at the Groden Center over the years with hundreds of children and adults with ASD. Their techniques have been perfected and honed in dozens of classrooms, work settings, and homes. This is critical. There is now a proliferation of books on how to work with people with ASD. Unfortunately many of these works, while sometimes interesting or provocative, are often relatively untested. In contrast, June Groden and her colleagues have taken the time and enormous effort to evaluate and refine their work, making your success with these techniques much more likely.

This is a very practical book. After introducing concepts such as resilience or self-efficacy the authors provide very clear, practical, and fun exercises as well as instructions for how to introduce these tasks and ensure that they are successful. For example, they describe a program they have used successfully over the years to help build confidence as well as creativity (the My Own World program). They developed these photography lessons for people with ASD to help them foster resilience and self-worth. As for all the exercises, the book describes in great detail the necessary steps to teach photography skills (e.g., placing the strap around your neck, aiming the camera, taking photographs, and, for advanced students, how to use a computer to improve and print photos).

You are about to be introduced to the future. Throughout the pages of this book are glimpses into the next generation of teaching goals for individuals with ASD, where the aim is not only to improve skills but to help the individuals become more confident and successful in life. The Groden Center is leading the field in showing us all how to fulfill that very important wish held by all parents – to help their child become happier. You are in for a treat!

V. Mark Durand, Ph.D.
Professor of Psychology
Co-Editor, Journal of Positive Behavior Interventions

CONTRIBUTORS

NARRATIVE WRITERS

Ayelet Kantor, Ph.D.
Leslie Weidenman, Ph.D.
Cooper R. Woodard, Ph.D.
June Groden, Ph.D.
Mary Pendergast, M.Ed.
Gregory Handel, Ph.D.
Deborah Alavosius, M.S.

RESEARCH AND ACTIVITY CONTRIBUTORS

Tenley Allard, B.A.
Demi Caris, B.S.
Jane Carlson, Ph.D.
Amy Diller, M.S.
Sage Goodwin, M.A.
Elaine Goudreau, M.Ed.
Jane Hesser, M.F.A., M.S.W., L.C.S.W.
Ann Miller, M.S.W.
Linda Ollari, A.S.
Nicole Perry, M.Ed.
Jacqueline Rastella, M.A.
Amy Rice, B.S.
Robin Ringer, M.Ed.
Debra Romano
Rick Smith, B.S.
Richard Spratt, M.A., C.A.G.S.
Lorna Swanson, B.S., B.A.
Krista Swiader, B.F.A.
. . . and all the classroom staff at the Groden Center.

Introduction and Assessing Positive Traits

> Imagine a science that is as interested in health and well-being as disease and disorder. A science that strives to promote flourishing and fulfillment at each of the individual, group, and social levels. A science that studies what makes life worth living. A science that holds meaningful lessons for all who choose to consider it. A science that speaks to us personally, as practitioners, as much as it does to the people for whom we practice. This is the science of positive psychology. (Linley and Joseph 2004, p.xv)

Traits such as optimism, resilience, and kindness are central topics in the growing field of positive psychology. This book addresses the importance of fostering these and other character strengths in persons with autism and developmental disabilities to improve their quality of life. Although there are many programs devoted to supporting this population, a focus on building traits within the realm of positive psychology has traditionally not been explored. In this introduction, we begin with a discussion of positive psychology to introduce the reader to this field and then present a historical perspective of treatment for persons with autism and developmental disabilities. We then discuss how this approach offers a new perspective in supporting persons with developmental disabilities, has the potential to improve quality of life, and has heuristic value in the development of new assessment and intervention technologies. We feel that this volume should appeal to a broad range of people from professionals in the areas of psychology, psychiatry, speech and language, special education, occupational therapy, physical therapy, and social work, to parents, caretakers, and staff at residential and day programs. In other words, there is something for everyone.

WHAT IS POSITIVE PSYCHOLOGY?

Seligman *et al.* (2005) define positive psychology as 'an umbrella term for the study of positive emotions, positive character traits, and enabling institutions' (p.410). With its roots found in earlier, growth-oriented works (e.g., Maslow 1971; Rogers 1951), positive psychology focuses on what is healthy and strength-oriented within people, and how these elements help us not only to cope more effectively, but also to flourish and become more adaptable in a world of challenges. Positive psychology functions from a strength-based rather than a deficit or pathology-based foundation, where the primary focus is on augmenting positive personal traits to maximize meaning and engagement in life, as well as positive emotional states. It has been evolving and expanding since the mid-1990s, and has brought together a vast array of literature and research topics. Researchers and other supporters of positive psychology have earned section status within the American Psychological Association's (APA) Division 17 (Society of Counseling Psychology) and have also generated enough research to merit a comprehensive handbook (Snyder and Lopez 2002).

In 2000, the *American Psychologist* (Anderson 2000) devoted a special issue to positive psychology, calling for a reconceptualization of how psychologists understand pathology and promote wellness. The opening article by Seligman and Csikszentmihalyi (2000) introduced the movement as a way to 'catalyze a change in the focus of psychology from preoccupation only with repairing the worst things in life to also building positive qualities' (p.5). As such, positive psychology is about living a quality life by maintaining psychological health and well-being, and fostering hope for the future. It is about having a life that is meaningful, and developing character traits that lead to good attitudes and feelings, such as courage, perseverance, self-control, resilience, and forgiveness. Positive psychology concerns itself with creating and nurturing wisdom, altruism, kindness, tolerance, and the capacity to love and give freely of one's self. Further, many positive psychology traits relate to prevention as they serve to buffer the damaging effects of experience, personal challenges, and mental illness. A traumatic or otherwise damaging event may become an opportunity for growth and development, if one possesses enough of the needed qualities. As Seligman and Csikszentmihalyi (2000) suggest, positive psychology's focus is to 'reorient psychology back to its two neglected missions – making normal people stronger and more productive and making high human potential actual' (p.8).

Many professionals who support persons with autism and developmental disabilities have, much like other practitioners in psychology, worked in accordance with more of a pathology- or deficit-based model. This approach often focuses on external observable behavior. Our main targets for change are the thinking patterns, self-images, attributions, and cognitive constructs that lead to happiness and well-being. By building on character strengths and incorporating both internal and external events, parents, teachers, caregivers, and therapists may be able to address more of the many aspects that create quality of life and a sense of well-being in persons with autism and developmental disabilities.

The result of this approach is a more comprehensive whole-person set of externally and internally directed interventions that may equip this population with a wider array of resources to cope with both unusual and everyday events. In short, fostering positive psychology traits in persons with autism and developmental disabilities builds upon external supports by improving the various ways they think about themselves, the people and world around them, and what is happening or may happen in the future to them. Keyes and Lopez (2002, p.51) capture this concept in stating that 'views of clients as "passive receptacles"…have become antiquated,' which highlights the essential need to incorporate a child's or adult's active participation in his or her own growth.

HISTORICAL PERSPECTIVES ON DEVELOPMENTAL DISABILITIES

There have been many changes in the field of developmental disabilities since the 1960s. In the late 1960s and early 1970s, Nirje (1969) and Wolfensberger (1972) authored papers on the topic of normalization that had lasting impact on the service delivery to persons with developmental disabilities. A completely new way of offering services to persons with developmental disabilities evolved from this philosophy. In the decades that followed, large institutions were closed and mainstreaming and inclusion became part of the school and community environments. Concurrent with these systems changes, researchers began to develop behavioral procedures including the application of learning theory to demonstrate how behaviors could be shaped or altered (Baer, Peterson and Sherman 1967). The efficacy of such interventions led to the creation of planned programs that use principles of learning to increase desired behaviors, and remediate unwanted behavioral challenges by focusing mainly on the alteration of consequential events. As the relationship between environmental conditions and behavior became more evident, research on functional assessment and functional analysis increased dramatically (Anderson and Freeman 2000; Groden 1989). The goal of assessing function was to identify the purpose of certain behaviors. New medications with fewer side effects were also developed, inclusion became a familiar term, and research in autism and developmental disabilities expanded. These forces all combined to enable persons with developmental disabilities to participate more fully in community life.

During this period, some organizations targeted inner behavior (thinking, feeling, images, and other private events) in addition to external behavioral processes. The Groden Center, for example, is an educational and treatment center for persons with autism and developmental disabilities, founded in 1976 in the midst of these sweeping changes. From its inception, the Groden Center promoted the inclusion of persons with developmental disabilities through education, vocational training, and residential living. In addition to focusing on community participation, inclusion, and using well-established behavioral techniques, the Center's main focus was (and continues to be) to improve the quality of life for the population it serves. In 1976, while acknowledging the benefits of a traditional behavioral model, the philosophy at the Groden Center also emphasized the importance of self-control (Groden, Baron, and Cautela 1988) and the inclusion of inner behavior in its treatment programs.

Procedures such as relaxation training (Cautela and Groden 1978), imagery, picture rehearsal, and stress reduction (Groden *et al.* 1994), and the stress survey scale (Groden *et al.* 2001) were developed and adapted for persons with autism and developmental disabilities, and were routinely integrated into their daily schedules and activities. The relaxation response could be prompted or accessed during identified stressful or challenging times, and imagery-based procedures including picture rehearsal using scripted scenes promoted self-control (Groden and Cautela 1984, 1988).

By reaping the treatment benefits of learning theory applications and also targeting inner behavior with innovative techniques, the children and adults at the Groden Center learned self-control by using relaxation and their practiced imagery scenes. These students have become active participants in their growth, a hallmark of the growing field of positive psychology but one rarely found in the field of autism and developmental disabilities. As we look to the future, we are able to focus on procedures that could foster the creation of the positive emotional states and ability to cope more effectively with challenging or negative events.

AN EMPHASIS ON VALUES

The application of positive psychology to persons with autism and developmental disabilities offers teachers, parents, and other caregivers an opportunity to look at their students, children, and adults from a new perspective. In addition to designing programs that decrease inappropriate behaviors and increase desired behaviors, developing interventions to foster positive traits shifts the emphasis from specific targeted behaviors to values. By looking at values, the horizons of programming can be expanded. For example, if a child destroys community property, in addition to targeting property destruction, caregivers also could focus on a long-term value of being a constructive and integrated member of the community. To achieve this, interventions might reinforce kind, empathetic, and courageous behavior, as well as foster optimistic thinking. Such traits assist in the development of a person's quality of life, and allow a person to be able to enjoy what school, community, and family life have to offer. Generally, a person who has traits such as kindness, courage, self-esteem, optimism, and resilience is someone whom others like to be with. In addition, people with these traits will have more opportunities provided for them, and will be able to engage more fully in a wider variety of life experiences. They may also respond more favorably to challenges and/or failures.

Approaches to foster character strengths should invoke a wide range of therapeutic techniques, with an emphasis on multi-modal (direct programming, incidental teaching, environmental conditions) and multi-sensory (visual, auditory, and kinesthetic) procedures. Based on simplified, adapted versions of interventions used for typically developing peers, techniques can be designed that have visual supports, have repeated practice, and use high levels of reinforcement. Strategies to promote generalization across settings are also recommended, including video and social modeling that can be carried out in group learning situations.

This book selects positive psychology procedures described in the literature for typical children and adults and makes adaptations suitable for use with persons with autism and developmental disabilities. These procedures form a starting point from which the reader may discover new ways to incorporate these programs into the general curriculum and treatment programs for the population with autism and other developmental disabilities. Such practices can impact community, home, and personal domains and can produce individuals who are more autonomous, self-confident, independent, and adaptable, and lead to the ultimate goal of improved well-being and quality of life. The implications of this approach are far-reaching, impacting curricula, teacher and parent training, and the definition of quality of life for this population. Rather than providing additional external supports or creating accommodating environments, the proposed multi-modal and multi-sensory perspective and interventions build positive and protective character strengths. This approach fosters personal resources within the person, which are essential to creating well-being and the pride associated with creating one's own happiness.

For this volume, we have chosen five character traits: optimism, humor, self-efficacy, kindness, and resilience. The book is divided into two parts. The first part contains a description of each character trait, along with a review of the literature, and the rationale for building this trait. The second part contains activities to foster each of these traits. All pages in the activity chapters that are marked with a ✓ are available in large format for download at www.jkp.com/catalogue/book/9781849058537/resources.

The contributors are all directors or supervisors at the Groden Center who have Masters or Ph.D. degrees, and many years of hands-on experience in providing treatment and educational services to a population with autism, other developmental disabilities, and challenging behaviors. The activities have been field tested in the classrooms at the Groden Center and at supervisor trainings. There are special chapters added to this book which we feel will be helpful to our readers. These include the ASPeCT Scale (Woodard 2006; see Table I.1), the Groden Center Photography Program, and descriptions of some of the terms and methods that we have used throughout the book.

ASPECT SCALE – ASSESSMENT SCALE FOR POSITIVE CHARACTER TRAITS

Our aim is to provide the groundwork for parents, teachers, caregivers, therapists, and administrators to begin to focus on the character traits described and then use the activities as springboards to build these traits with their own children and adults. The ASPeCT Scale (Woodard 2006; see Table I.1) can be given first as a pre-test to determine priority areas to teach.

Table I.1 Assessment Scale for Positive Character Traits – Developmental Disabilities (ASPeCT-DD)

Client name: ....

Rater: ....

Date: .....   Age of client: .....   How long have you known client? .....

Directions: Please rate each item by circling the number that best describes the client at the current time, as compared to peers with similar levels of functioning. Use the following scale:

1 = **Not at all** characteristic of this person

2 = **A little** characteristic of this person

3 = **Somewhat** characteristic of this person

4 = **Very** characteristic of this person

5 = **Extremely** characteristic of this person

	1	2	3	4	5
1. I think this person is courageous.	1	2	3	4	5
2. This person is bothered, concerned, or upset when someone else is uncomfortable or distressed.	1	2	3	4	5
3. This person has a nice sense of humor.	1	2	3	4	5
4. This person can be thoughtful and helpful to others.	1	2	3	4	5
5. This person does not hold a grudge against others.	1	2	3	4	5
6. This person shows caring for other people.	1	2	3	4	5
7. This person can accept when he or she has made a mistake.	1	2	3	4	5
8. This person shows kindness to others.	1	2	3	4	5
9. When I am sad, this person responds to my feelings with concern.	1	2	3	4	5
10. This person tries to solve his or her problems.	1	2	3	4	5

11. This person does not lose his or her temper. *I*	1	2	3	4	5
12. Even when this person is afraid, he or she tries to do what is right or expected of him or her. *I*	1	2	3	4	5
13. This person shows a sensitivity to the needs and feelings of others. *I*	1	2	3	4	5
14. This person 'bounces back' easily. *E*	1	2	3	4	5
15. This person is generally able to control him/ herself. *I*	1	2	3	4	5
16. I think this person generally expects good things to happen to him or her. *N*	1	2	3	4	5
17. This person uses humor to cope with difficulties. *E*	1	2	3	4	5
18. This person shows thanks for help from others. *N*	1	2	3	4	5
19. I think this person is happy. *N*	1	2	3	4	5
20. Even when things are hard, this person keeps on trying. *N*	1	2	3	4	5
21. This person tries to follow directions. *I*	1	2	3	4	5
22. This person seems to enjoy life and is thankful for life's simple pleasures. *I*	1	2	3	4	5
23. This person gets over his or her mistakes in a reasonable amount of time. *E*	1	2	3	4	5
24. This person does not try to retaliate or get back at others who have hurt him or her. *I*	1	2	3	4	5
25. This person usually thinks things will go his or her way. *E*	1	2	3	4	5
26. It is fairly easy for this person to make new friends. *F*	1	2	3	4	5

Developed at the Groden Center by Cooper R. Woodard, June Groden, and Matthew Goodwin

The scale provides a measure to assess the strength of a wide range of character traits. The areas showing deficits should become priorities for intervention. For more information on this scale, see Chapter 12 in this book, which is devoted to the ASPeCT Scale. We hope that this book will motivate others to initiate research and help to expand this literature in the field of autism and developmental disabilities and positive psychology.

Chapter 1

Optimism

Figure 1.1 Students who participate in the Special Olympics are encouraged to focus on positive outcomes

WHAT IS OPTIMISM?

In the field of psychology, optimism has been a topic of research for many years. Investigators have examined ways to define and measure it, looked at the differences between optimistic and pessimistic people, and explored theories about how optimism develops in individuals and is fostered by their experiences. Optimism is also a familiar concept and commonly used word. Most people believe it has something to do with maintaining a positive outlook, expecting that positive things will happen, and behaving as if anticipating a good outcome. Dictionaries confirm this. *The American Heritage Dictionary of the English Language* (2006), for example, defines optimism as 'a tendency to expect the best possible outcome or to dwell on the most hopeful aspects of a situation.' The student in Figure 1.1 takes part in Special Olympics because she expects good things to happen, and they do!

Martin Seligman, co-author of *The Optimistic Child*, defines the fundamentals of optimism as the following:

> The basis of optimism does not lie in positive phrases or images of victory, but in the *way* you think about *causes*. Each of us has habits of thinking about causes, a personality trait I call 'explanatory style.' Explanatory style develops in childhood, and without explicit intervention is lifelong. (Seligman *et al.* 1995, p.54; emphasis added)

Seligman *et al.* (1995) describes the three crucial dimensions of explanatory style which children use to explain why any particular good or bad event happens. These dimensions are labeled as *permanence, pervasiveness,* and *personalization,* with each dimension referring to beliefs on a continuum from extreme optimism to extreme pessimism. The dimensions are described in this way:

- *Permanence* addresses whether a person believes that the cause of a bad event is permanent, that is, never changing (the pessimistic view), or temporary (the optimistic view).

- *Pervasiveness* has to do with the individual's belief about the extent of the problem, whether it is global and affects everything (the pessimistic view) or specific and affects only one thing (the optimistic view).

- *Personalization* addresses a person's view of whose fault it is that a negative event occurred.

Seligman *et al.* (1995) use the term *general self-blame* in reference to the pessimist's view that it is some generalized personal flaw or characteristic that is the cause of the problem. The optimist's view is called *behavioral self-blame*, as the optimist typically assigns blame to a particular behavior or action, not a personality characteristic or flaw. For example, a student with a pessimistic explanatory style who receives a bad grade on a test might conclude that the grade was a result of being stupid. An optimistic child in the same situation would be more likely to conclude the bad grade was a result of not studying hard enough.

Carver and Gaines (1987) of the University of Miami write that optimism and pessimism concern people's expectations for the future. When facing challenges, optimists are more apt to be confident that they will succeed, even when progress is slow. They also note that optimists are likely to experience a more positive mix of feelings than pessimists as they tackle difficult situations. In an article for the National Cancer Institute, Carver (no date) suggests that optimism is related to, but not identical to self-efficacy.

Carver suggests that in self-efficacy, people believe it is their personal efforts or skills that will determine a positive outcome; in optimism, people could have many reasons why they think an outcome could be positive. Using the example of overcoming the side effects of chemotherapy, self-efficacious people who believe they have the strength to overcome the effects of chemotherapy will struggle harder to do so. Optimists take a broader view and may believe that they will overcome chemotherapy's side effects, citing their wonderful oncologist, saying they are blessed, noting they have the support of friends and family and they are strong. For Carver, the positive, optimistic feelings are not solely due to the belief in one's personal abilities but rather a collection of supportive and positive components.

RATIONALE FOR FOCUSING ON OPTIMISM

Much research has been done on the level of optimism people have when faced with difficult situations or stressful life events. Human responses to familiar life challenges, such as caring for a loved one with a serious disease, going through a major life change (moving, divorce, death of a family member), having a significant illness, or being the survivor of a violent event or other life trauma have been studied extensively.

In general, the results of these studies have shown that optimistic people tend to:

- *Enjoy better psychological and physiological health.* Optimists are generally less likely to become depressed and have an increased sense of well-being, which often translates into positive outcomes across a range of life domains (Carver and Gaines 1987; Gladstone and Kaslow 1995; Segerstrom 2005). This effect can be explained by the fact that optimistic individuals are less threatened and defeated by adverse events, obstacles, and hassles (Lazarus 1991).

- *Use a wider range of effective coping strategies.* Optimists employ a variety of positive strategies, such as problem solving, humor, acceptance, and reframing when faced with challenges. Reframing is a way of looking at negative events and finding their positive elements, or identifying the positive outcomes that may result from those events (e.g., viewing missing a bus as an opportunity to get a cup of coffee and finish up an assignment). This optimistic style of thinking supports effective problem solving. When pessimists are faced with problems, they tend to employ inefficient, non-productive, avoidance-oriented coping strategies, such as blaming themselves (Cunningham, Brandon and Frydenberg 2002; Nes and Segerstrom 2006). In addition, pessimists may get depressed, deny there is a problem, ignore the problem, or try to escape it altogether (Nes and Segerstrom 2006). In extreme situations, the pessimist's repertoire of coping strategies may include excessive spending, eating, drinking alcohol, or using drugs.

- *Feel that they have fewer barriers in fulfilling their goals.* Optimistic individuals generally have more confidence and motivation when it pertains to reaching their desired goals. They also believe they have fewer external barriers (such as lack of resources) that would get in the way of accomplishing their goals. For example, female students who are more optimistic tend to be more decisive regarding their careers than their pessimistic peers (Creed, Patton and Bartrum 2004).

- *Benefit more from social support in times of stress.* In general, optimists are more approachable, create fewer emotional burdens for their supporters and, with their positive attitude, motivate supporters to keep in close contact with them (Brissette, Scheier and Carver 2002; Snyder 2002).

HOW TO NURTURE OPTIMISM

Cognitive-behavioral therapies offer an effective style of intervention for helping individuals be more optimistic. One of the goals of therapy is to help individuals become aware of their unrealistic, negative self-talk in the face of challenges and how these are ineffective and damaging to the explanatory style. For example, the person who concludes, 'I can't do anything right,' when attempting a new task is engaging in negative self-talk. It is linked to the pervasive dimension of the explanatory style because a general, wide-reaching assessment is being made and the effect is not a positive one. This type of awareness training is coupled with teaching individuals how to replace negative thoughts with more accurate statements of their abilities, and the steps needed to be successful. Cognitive therapies also address the thinking and behavioral styles individuals use in response to challenges, problem-solving skills, and the means of building supportive social networks (Reivich et al. 2005).

A pessimistic cognitive style, as we have discussed, can be a source of distress for the individual. This is particularly true when the person is exposed to a stressful scenario. In such situations, negative thoughts automatically propose a pessimistic view of the situation. For example, a person with a pessimistic cognitive style might draw the wrong conclusion about why two busy peers who are talking to each other do not turn to offer a greeting when he or she enters the room. The pessimist may interpret the lack of greeting as a snub, or might conclude that he or she is generally disliked. A cognitive therapeutic intervention would attempt to help individuals with pessimistic styles recognize when their thoughts or perspectives are inaccurate, improbable, or dysfunctional (Seligman et al. 1995). Programs aimed toward children sometimes use the terms *helpful* and *unhelpful* to guide children in discriminating between optimistic and pessimistic thought styles (Barrett, Sonderegger and Xenos 2003; Seligman et al. 1995).

CHANGING EXPLANATORY STYLE

Why is explanatory style so important? Seligman *et al.* (1995) suggest that the person's beliefs about adversity dictate particular emotional and behavioral consequences. His model is based on Ellis's (1962) cognitive therapy, ABC model, in which:

A = Adversity (any negative event)

B = Belief (or explanatory style)

C = Consequence (feelings and behavior after the adversity)

The model proposes that an adverse event leads to beliefs that in turn affect the consequences or the individual's response(s) to the event.

How an individual's beliefs or explanatory style affect mood and disposition is illustrated in the following example:

> Jack desperately wants a key role in the school play. After getting his hopes up that he would get the lead, he instead receives a smaller role (A = adversity). If he thinks of himself as a failure because he didn't get the part he wished for (B = belief), it is likely that he will feel badly about himself and his mood may become depressed (C = consequence). By viewing himself as a failure, Jack is using a pessimistic explanation in confronting the adversity of not getting the lead part in the play. His future behavior may be affected by his pessimistic style. For example, in the rehearsals, he might act out, sulk, or behave in an insecure manner. If, however, Jack tells himself, 'That's okay, you can't always get the part you want,' or positively *reframes* the situation by telling himself, 'I guess it is good that I do not have the lead role, because I am a better singer and I have a part with lots of songs,' chances are he will enjoy participating in the play in the lesser role without becoming depressed.

Table 1.1 outlines pessimistic and optimistic explanations of this adverse event along the three crucial dimensions of Seligman's theory of explanatory style: *permanence, pervasiveness,* and *personalization.*

Seligman *et al.* (1995) field tested a program developed to promote optimism in middle school aged children at risk for developing depression in a number of school systems. Seligman's findings form the basis of the book *The Optimistic Child* (Seligman *et al.* 1995).

Table 1.1 Summary of Seligman's dimensions of explanatory style for a sample adverse event: failing to get the lead role in a school play

Pessimistic explanations	Optimistic explanations
Dimension: **Permanence**	
Permanent 'I will never be in a leading role!'	**Temporary** 'Next year I will be in a higher grade and may get the leading role.'
Dimension: **Pervasiveness**	
Pervasive 'I am such a loser! I will never succeed in anything!'	**Specific** 'People didn't notice me in the auditions, but I can show my talents later during the play.' or 'I am a much better singer than an actor. I can try for the singing parts.'
Dimension: **Personalization**	
Personal 'I am a terrible actor.' or 'Mrs. Ronald hates me! She doesn't want to give me any part I like!'	**Impersonal** 'That's okay, everybody wants this part and the teacher can't give it to everybody.'

The program begins by helping students identify the ABCs – adversities, beliefs, and consequences. The second step is to help individual students identify their own explanatory styles or beliefs about adversities. This is often done through exercises in which students read scenarios which present an adversity, and the character explains why he or she believes it occurred.

In this activity, the students learn how different hypothetical explanations regarding previous adverse events that have occurred can affect the character's overall mood and expectations. Later, they are asked to label the explanations on Seligman's three dimensions of explanatory style – permanence, pervasiveness, and personalization. The students then learn to assess the attributions they make about adverse events in their lives and come up with alternative optimistic explanations for them. Seligman is training students to consider more optimistic explanations, instead of automatically adapting thinking patterns reflective of pessimism. The final step of the program involves teaching goal setting, decision making, creative problem solving, assertiveness and negotiation training, to reduce feelings of helplessness, and to handle adversities more effectively when they arise.

OPTIMISM IN AUTISM

Many of the characteristics of individuals with autism, such as difficulty with social interactions and communication, anxiety, and rigidity and a desire for sameness, increase their vulnerability to life challenges. Individuals with autism spectrum disorders often report extreme sensitivity to environmental and sensory stimuli, difficulty dealing with disruptions to expected routines, anxiety, stress, and problems negotiating a social world that can be very confusing (Groden *et al.* 2001). Their difficulties are reflected in higher levels of depression, anxiety, paranoia, and phobias compared to the general population (Barnhill and Myles 2001; Bellini 2004; Blackshaw *et al.* 2001). Fostering an optimistic perspective and alternatives to past behavioral patterns in individuals with autism may provide increased capacity to cope with challenging situations and circumstances. Promoting a positive explanatory style could increase successful problem solving, decrease a sense of helplessness and ineffective coping, and foster a more positive coping style and a world view that could be beneficial.

NURTURING OPTIMISM IN THE CLASSROOM

The Groden Center's curriculum to promote optimism in children with autism and other developmental disabilities uses the theoretical base offered by Seligman to promote positive explanatory styles for challenging events and adversities.

The goals of the program are for students to:

- change attributions and beliefs regarding specific adverse events
- emphasize positive aspects of their lives to support a general optimistic outlook.

Listed below are four methods to foster optimism in the classroom.

Modeling

One of the best ways to promote an optimistic environment in the classroom is by modeling optimistic thinking and explanatory styles throughout the day. Many individuals are optimistic by nature. However, it is not a given that every teacher, therapist, volunteer, resource specialist, and consultant who works with individuals with autism will have an optimistic outlook. Understanding the importance of optimistic thinking and the ways it can be fostered will enable all those working with the students to incorporate optimism into their own actions and teaching. This can be done throughout the day if teachers are aware of explanatory styles and alert to opportunities to address them. As challenging situations arise, teachers can model how to handle them in an optimistic manner by verbalizing optimistic beliefs.

For example, if a preferred activity is cancelled, the teacher could say something like, 'Even though we can't go to the library, I bet we can find something fun to do together in the classroom,' and then solicit ideas from the students for a positive replacement activity. Or, the teacher could ask students to create other optimistic thoughts. Along with the initial training on the importance of creating an optimistic environment, teachers should receive feedback regarding their use of optimistic explanations, monitor their own comments, and avoid any displays of pessimism.

Video modeling also can be used to promote optimism. With video modeling, students observe videotapes of themselves or others engaging in positive role-plays in which optimistic explanatory styles are acted out in the face of challenges. Reading books with optimistic themes (e.g., *The Little Engine That Could* (Piper 1930), a story of an engine whose motto was 'I think I can') and watching movies or television shows that present individuals overcoming adversity are other ways of modeling optimism for students.

Positive scanning

Encouraging classroom-wide positive scanning is another way of promoting optimism. This could be done at the start of the day or perhaps during a morning group activity. For example, students could review with their teacher the activities or events they are looking forward to for that day. Initially, teachers might have to prompt students with comments or questions like, 'Think of the fun things you will do today,' or 'What might happen today that you like to do?' Answers could be recorded in a journal, on a blackboard or other format. At the end of the day, the teacher could review the items with the students in an effort to show that many of the anticipated positive events actually happened. This is also a good time to discuss unexpected positive events that occurred over the course of the day.

Positive affirmations

Having a child review positive affirmations individually or in a group setting is another way of creating an optimistic environment. The affirmations can be general positive statements such as, 'Good things happen to me,' and 'School is fun.' Or, they can be more specific comments linked to causal statements (e.g., 'My friends like to be with me because I say nice things about them'). The causal statement reinforces the idea that good things are likely to occur because of qualities or actions the child controls, not simply by chance. For example, a student might affirm, 'I'm good at sports because I always try my hardest.'

Cognitive picture rehearsal

Individuals with autism often deal with gaps in understanding by guessing the reasons why things occur (Meyer *et al.* 2006). If their explanations are negative, it is important to teach them to evaluate their thinking more reasonably and create alternative ideas. Cognitive picture rehearsal scenes or sequences address the optimistic explanation associated with the situation, stressor, or aversive event depicted, and add an optimistic problem-solving strategy. This strategy is effective for students with limited insight, problem-solving and communication skills.

These four methods are not an exhaustive list. There are undoubtedly countless variations and combinations of these strategies that can be designed to foster optimism. In presenting these ideas, we are interested in stimulating our readers to add to the list of suggestions and encourage teachers, parents, and other caregivers to foster an optimistic outlook.

Chapter 2

Humor

Figure 2.1 Understanding humor is to enjoy incongruence

WHAT IS HUMOR?

Humor is the playful recognition, enjoyment, and/or creation of incongruity. Although it might be strange or even frightening to some at first, continuous exposure can help students with autism learn to enjoy incongruence and express joy, as seen in Figure 2.1. It is the quality that makes something laughable or amusing (Peterson and Seligman 2004). Individuals who demonstrate a sense of humor have the ability to reflect on what is amusing, comical, absurd, or incongruous by laughing, joking, or having a jovial attitude and generally positive philosophy of life.

Therapeutic humor is any intervention which uses humorous techniques, whether intentionally or spontaneously, to increase self-understanding, improve behavior, and enhance overall health and wellness. By stimulating a playful discovery, expression, and appreciation of the absurdity or incongruity of life's situations, the individual and the therapist or teacher gain shared positive emotional experiences and improve their rapport and connection with each other (Association for Applied and Therapeutic Humor 2005; Franzini 2001).

RATIONALE FOR FOCUSING ON HUMOUR

Why humor? Persons working with individuals with autism focus on nurturing the development of many skills. When considering the many benefits of humor, including its positive impact on cognition, socialization, and health, we realize the importance of teaching and cultivating this skill. In this chapter, we consider the many positive effects of humor and how it is both possible and important to foster its use among individuals with autism.

Why is humor important? Humor is a fundamental aspect of social interaction. Most of us experience humor without being aware of its many benefits. Research on humor highlights these benefits, providing the incentives for teaching humor and the appreciation of humor.

Humor complements cognitive development. Humor, cognition, and emotional development are mutual processes, synergistically affecting one another. These relationships can be demonstrated by the following example:

Two-year-old Michelle laughs as she observes a cow puppet opening its mouth and saying 'Meow.' Michelle finds this funny because she is able to use and generalize her acquired knowledge about animal sounds to anticipate that a cow sound will be 'Moo.' She understands the difference between the way things are reported and the way they are supposed to be. When the cow instead says 'Meow,' Michelle is quickly able to make a comparison between the expected and the actual, concluding that this is a mistake. It is incongruent. Michelle's cognitive abilities allow her to process the incongruity and respond with laughter. She also relies on her emotional processing capabilities to enjoy the discrepancy without becoming upset or confused. Michelle's appropriate humor response relies on general knowledge, critical judgment, imagination, and flexibility to enjoy the incongruence.

Humor fosters social connections (Zillman 1977). Social interactions such as college reunions or work meetings can often be both enjoyable and stressful. In such circumstances, we will often turn to humor to relieve both anticipated and actual stress.

In social situations, humor can alleviate stress in many different ways. For example, humor can be an ice breaker in new or uncomfortable situations, and it can bring people together by sharing a laugh. The presence of humor in social interaction can foster a sense of ease and comfort among participants. As one might expect, socially adept individuals tend to possess a well-developed sense of humor. A study of young adults found that those who had a better developed sense of humor also had more effective communication and social skills, increased capacity for intimacy, and fewer interpersonal conflicts (Kuiper and Martin 1998).

Individuals with autism are frequently challenged by anxiety and by stress responses when confronted with social demands. Cultivating a capacity for understanding and using humor in social situations has the potential to promote participation and reduce stress associated with social demands.

Humor is a coping skill associated with the use of other coping skills. Individuals who have a developed sense of humor are less affected by stressful life events and exhibit less anxiety and negative moods (Kuiper and Martin 1998; Prerost 1988). Along with the ability to use humor, these individuals tend to have additional and complementary coping skills that include positive reframing/changing perspectives, acknowledging positive outcomes, and reducing dysfunctional attitudes (Lefcourt and Thomas 1998).

Humor eases communication around tough issues. Humor is a socially accepted way to provide criticism and illustrate illogical or irrational thinking (Franzini 2000; Prerost 1988, 1989). Humor is also used to overcome the fear of criticism which provokes anxiety, embarrassment, and degradation. Laughing at our own weaknesses, ridiculing our mistakes, joking about our senior moments helps others and ourselves accept these ineptitudes gracefully (Nilsen and Nilsen 1999). All of us rely on humor to mitigate the stress of handling difficult subjects and situations, and individuals with autism who have a developed understanding of humor can use this strategy.

Humor supports learning. Research suggests (Nilsen and Nilsen 1987, 1999; Schacht and Stewart 1990) that when incorporating humor into the class and the school curriculum, students may benefit from increased:

- focus and attention
- rapport with the teachers
- flexibility, creativity, and complex thinking
- interest in the material taught
- interpersonal skills and socialization
- problem-solving capabilities
- physical and emotional relaxation
- comfort with academic demands (tests, etc.).

Also, humor increases alertness, and therefore has a potentially beneficial effect on learning in individuals who are challenged by sub-optimal alertness (hypo and hyper reactivity to stimulation), as is often the case in individuals with autism and sensory integration problems.

Humor improves health and has an established role as a complementary treatment. It can support recovery and coping. Humor increases the release of endorphins, modulates endocrine system function, improves immunological system responsivity, and affects psychological and physical well-being (Franzini 2001; Lefcourt and Thomas 1998).

Individuals with autism are known to have a reduced tolerance for stress due to their frequently limited repertoire of coping strategies (Groden and Cautela 1984; Groden *et al.* 1994). Those who support individuals with autism during times of stress, physical illness, or in the management of chronic health problems, should consider how they can infuse humor into these situations and teach the child to do so as well.

Incorporating humor into the life of individuals with autism can benefit their well-being. Teaching humor as a source of joy and as a coping strategy is especially important given studies showing higher levels of anxiety and depression among individuals on the spectrum (Kim *et al.* 2000). Humorous and positive reframing strategies may enable them to cope better, recover from and manage challenging life experiences, confront difficult circumstances like illness, failures, or transitions, and communicate about difficult subjects. Those of us who live with and teach individuals with autism should strive to ensure that they have opportunities, both formal and informal, to improve their ability to use and appreciate humor so they might also experience these important benefits. Continuous exposure will help students learn that the unexpected can be safe as well as funny, as seen in Figure 2.2. Humor comes less naturally to the person with autism, but it can be fostered and taught with the support of an informed and skillful teaching partner.

WHAT'S SO FUNNY? DEVELOPMENTAL STAGES OF HUMOR IN EARLY CHILDHOOD

A comprehensive theory concerning the developmental stages of humor derives from the work of Paul McGhee (Loizou 2006; McGhee 1984). McGhee identifies the comprehension and expression of humor through the different stages of physical and emotional development, paralleling Piaget's theory of cognitive development. A review of McGhee's stages of humor (see Table 2.1) indicates that the acquisition of humor is dependent on complex interrelated skills involving cognition, communication, and sensory capabilities.

HUMOR IN PEOPLE WITH AUTISM

The foundation of humor develops in the first and second years of life and is dependent on communication, play, and imagination. For individuals with autism, these requisite skills are often elusive. Even individuals with high-functioning autism and Asperger syndrome are found to have a less developed appreciation and comprehension of humor and humorous situations (Emerich *et al.* 2003). Though the capacity for understanding humor among individuals with autism is variable, simpler forms of humor (such as clowning and slapstick) tend to be more accessible than those that

Table 2.1 Humor developmental stages (based on McGhee 1976, 1984, 2003)

Piaget's stages of cognitive development	Humor stage	Age	Description
Sensorimotor	Stage 0: Laughter without humor	0–6 months	During this stage, individuals laugh at things that are physiologically arousing to them in a familiar non-threatening situation. Examples include being bounced on a knee, tickling, and other forms of tactile stimulation. Laughing at this stage is not related to humor.
Sensorimotor	Stage 1: Laughter at the attachment figure	6–12 or 15 months	This is perhaps an individual's earliest engagement with humor. Individuals react by laughing in response to the recognition of behaviors that are beyond the usual pattern. Examples include laughing when seeing others engage in exaggerated or silly behaviors like waddling like a penguin or making silly faces.
Sensorimotor moving into Preoperational	Stage 2: Object substitution	12 or 15 months to 3, 4, or 5 years	In this stage, children begin to engage in pretend play. They find the incongruency produced by using an object in an atypical way funny (using a bowl as a hat). It is in this stage that individuals begin to create humor, rather than just react to it.
Preoperational	Stage 3: Misnaming objects or actions	2 to 3 or 4 years	During this stage, budding language skills generate new opportunities for humor. Individuals think it is funny to call things by names that are wrong. The individual in this stage will create humor by calling a cat a dog, calling mommy daddy, etc. Another expression of humor is the misnaming by using opposites. The individual in this stage will create humor by saying things like 'Ashes, ashes, we all fall up.'

Piagetian Stage	Humor Stage	Age	Description
Preoperational	Stage 4a: Playing with word sounds	3–5 years	Several new forms of humor emerge in this stage. Calling things by the wrong name continues to be funny, but a new way of playing with words also becomes funny. During this stage, word play is extended to playing with the way words sound. This often takes the form of repeating variations of a familiar word over and over, such as 'Daddy, faddy, paddy' or 'Silly, dilly, willy.'
Preoperational	Stage 4b: Nonsense real-world combinations	3–5 years	In addition to playing with sounds or words, many three-year-olds start putting real words together in nonsensical combinations known to be wrong. The following are typical of this type of humor: 'I want more tree milk,' or 'I have mailbox flower,' or 'I want peanut butter chair.'
Preoperational	Stage 4c: Distortion of features of objects, people, or animals	3–5 years	At this stage, individuals find it funnier to distort some aspect of their conceptual understanding of objects, rather than just calling them by the wrong name. The following are the most common forms of humor at this stage: adding features that don't belong (a dog's head on a person's body); removing features that do belong (a cat with no tail or legs); changing the shape, size, location, color, or length of familiar things (eyes and ears in reverse places); incongruous or impossible behavior (a cow on roller skates).
Preoperational moving into Concrete Operational	Stage 5a: Pre-riddle	5–6 or 7 years	In this stage, individuals become interested in the verbal humor they hear around them. They imitate telling riddles without always understanding them. Eventually they begin to understand the double meanings involved in puns as they move into the concrete operational thinking stage.
Concrete Operational moving into Formal Operational	Stage 5b: Riddles and jokes	7–11 years	Individuals in this stage start to use and enjoy the ambiguous meanings of words when they realize the connection between elements of the joke that initially seemed to be unrelated. They receive pleasure from understanding and creating a logical resolution of the incongruity within the joke, and are therefore capable of creating appropriate punch lines to riddles or jokes. They can also discriminate between riddles that make sense and ones that don't. The individual understands jokes based on concepts that he or she has mastered. Adult humor is an expansion, and a more complex form of stage 5.

Figure 2.2 During recess in the Groden Center playground, a staff member dressed as Red Fraggle (a character from the children's television series *Fraggle Rock*) helps students become comfortable with unusual appearances

rely on the ability to process incongruity and ambiguity or call upon an understanding or appreciation of another person's perceptions.

An inability to understand humor among individuals with autism can increase frustration and stress, and may even lead them to become victimized by humor that is beyond their capacity to comprehend. Close observation of individuals with autism shows that their production of humor, even when it occurs, is not often shared by others. When shared humor does happen, it is likely the result of the purposeful encouragement and modeling of humor over time.

NURTURING HUMOR IN INDIVIDUALS WITH AUTISM

The nurturing of humor in individuals with autism and developmental disabilities can be achieved by:

- ensuring that humor is appropriate to the individual's cognitive and emotional level of comprehension

- making humor a recurring part of daily life in the home and/or classroom

- providing interpretation and explanation during incidental exposure to humor to increase recognition, understanding, and appreciation

- teaching discrimination between what is real versus imaginary, funny versus not funny/hurtful, and serious versus not serious/ playful

- modeling an affective response to humor (laughter, animation, etc.).

Identifying the developmental level of an individual with autism is a critical first step when attempting to teach and nurture humor. Table 2.1 provides information which can assist parents and teachers in assessing a child's developmental humor level. Given that many individuals with autism are functioning at developmental stages below their age level, parents and teachers need to adapt their strategies accordingly to determine what humorous activities and topics are most comprehensible and suitable.

Once the developmental humor level is determined, the topics to be presented should be chosen. Topics that make people laugh are those which are not only relevant to their lives, but also slightly challenging to their emotions, thoughts, and expectations:

- *Relevancy:* the more relevant the subject is to an individual's personal experiences, the funnier it will be to the individual. Knowing a child's foods, activities, family traditions, or pets, for example, is an important aspect of identifying themes and topics that might be amusing to the child. Identifying humorous targets based on personal relevancy to a child or student will increase the likelihood that the humor will be understood, appreciated, and, possibly, replicated.

- *Cognitive challenge:* whether it is a simple word play or a joke based on a logical mistake, the audience should get it. If we need an explanation, we will be less likely to think of it as funny. If, on the other hand, the challenge is too obvious, we will also not find it funny.

For example, McGhee (1976) presented jokes that required an understanding of fractions and conservation concepts to school age children, ages 5, 6, and 11:

> Mr. Jones went into a restaurant and ordered a whole pizza for dinner. When the waiter asked if he wanted it cut into six or eight pieces, Mr. Jones said, 'Oh, you'd better make it six! I could never eat eight!' (p.422)

Humor based on knowledge of categories concepts went like this:

> 'Please stay out of the house today,' Susie's mother said. 'I have too much work to do.' 'OK,' said Susie, as she walked to the stairs. 'Where do you think you're going?' her mother asked. 'Well,' said Susie, 'If I can't stay in the house, I'll just play in my room instead.' (p.424)

Children who were challenged by the concept, but able to figure out the cognitive mistake, found it funny. However, children who had not yet acquired the requisite cognitive and academic skills did not find the humor in these jokes.

As well as being able to get the joke because it has relevancy and is consistent with a person's cognitive ability, there is the outward manifestation of appreciation and enjoyment that follows, typically laughter. The overt expression of laughter signals to others that you not only get the joke, but also find it humorous. For individuals with autism, the overt behavior of laughing might not follow, even if they understand the joke. Similarly, laughter may ensue because others are laughing, but the child may not know why. It is possible that modeling an affective response (laughter following a joke) will promote the individual to respond with laughter upon encountering future humorous situations.

TEACHING THE RULES OF HUMOR TO INDIVIDUALS WITH AUTISM

Individuals with autism are often limited in their ability to understand and respond to the social cues and customs which typical individuals rely upon to discern the difference between appropriate and inappropriate uses of humor. Given this problem, it is up to the parent or teacher of individuals with autism to convey the often subtle rules of humor related to topics, targets, and settings for jokes and silliness. Parents, teachers, and caregivers can relate the following rules to the child:

- If you love to tell jokes, just tell them. You can learn new jokes using books. You can also ask your parents, brothers, sisters, or watch fun T.V. shows and look at magazines to get ideas. When you have the joke you would like to tell, practice it with your family first.

- Your joke will be more successful if it is related to the activity, or to a holiday that is coming. For example, practice Halloween jokes around Halloween time, and not other times of the year.

- When you act silly, or tell a joke, look at those you are joking with. Watch to see if they are laughing. If they do not laugh, it might be because they do not think it is funny or they may have seen you act like that or heard the joke before. Try to avoid repeating the behavior or the joke with them, but try another joke at another time. Do not be discouraged if not everybody laughs at every joke.

- When trying to amuse others, it is important not to say or do anything at the expense of another's feelings.

THE ROLE OF PARENT AND TEACHER AS A SOURCE OF HUMOR

Respectful and appropriate humor has a legitimate place in a person's communicative repertoire, and a child with autism needs to be able to enjoy this aspect as well. Although it is frequently difficult for many adults to express low developmental levels of humor (such as waddling like a penguin in the classroom), most find that with a rationale behind it and lots of practice, they become comfortable expressing this type of playfulness. If people are not comfortable acting in a silly or playful manner, they can infuse their interactions and teaching style with animation and positive energy. Being animated helps people engage individuals with autism who have reduced situational and social awareness, and teaches them to attend to and read physical cues associated with processing humor (facial expressions, body movement, tone and inflection of voices, etc.). Ways to infuse humor and playfulness into an interactive style include the following:

- Be lively and exaggerate body movements when talking.

- Use different voices for characters when telling or reading a story.

- Develop visual or auditory signals that designate fun time, such as putting on a funny hat or ringing a bell. Whatever sign, symbol, or action is chosen, it should communicate that it is playtime and the children can be silly.

- Sing or hum funny songs.

- Talk through puppets using an animated voice and exaggerated movements.

- Reward and support appropriate humorous and fun behaviors initiated by the children.

- Laugh and play with them spontaneously.

- Act silly in order to teach problem-solving skills and let students help:

  Lori, a teacher of young individuals with autism, used humor to teach the daily living skill of packing for a day at the beach. She began with a large beach tote and an animated introduction, 'Wow, it is warm today! I think I will go to the beach. What should I pack?' She then picked up items one by one. 'I will need my swimsuit, sun block, mittens, and a scarf,' she said. Students responded to her mistakes with amusement. Lori then asked them what else she might need. Students offered correct responses such as 'You need a towel.' Lori responded with, 'Of course, silly me!'

The wide range of functioning within a classroom of children with autism means that not all students will achieve the same benefits from specific activities and lessons. The classroom teacher should recognize that humor is a positive force that will reach all of the learners on some level, directly or indirectly. Experiment, play, and have fun!

Parents and teachers should consider their own personalities as well as the individual social and behavioral characteristics of students when choosing strategies and activities to enhance their understanding and use of humor. Matching one's humor style to a child's cognitive, emotional, and developmental humor level can require significant creativity and labor, especially when it comes to planning structured lessons.

APPLICATION OF HUMOR IN THE HOME AND CLASSROOM

Increasing playfulness in daily home and classroom routines is perhaps the most fundamental and easiest way to begin cultivating a sense of humor. Humorous activities, in contrast to joke telling, can tap different levels of humor. Following are a number of strategies that can be incorporated easily into any classroom curricula or home environment to increase playfulness.

Story time

Include humorous and silly books in your library. Reading comical books with your child or student is a great way to introduce humor. Reading aloud enables the reader to interject animation, laugh when appropriate, and engage learners in identifying what is humorous about a story. Individuals with limited verbal comprehension may instead benefit from books of photographs that capture incongruency (dogs in tuxedos, babies in flower pots, etc.) or pictures that capture funny situations or angles. Given the extensive inventory of humorous books available for all age levels, it is possible to use books and story time as a strategy to comprehend humor. There are even silly stories that can be used to support academic lessons. *Cloudy with a Chance of Meatballs* by Judi Barrett is an example of a funny book that can be read as a complement to academic lessons on weather (see Chapter 7). Other recommended books and websites for story time activities are:

- Armstrong, Jennifer. *Once Upon a Banana*
- Arnold, Tedd. *No Jumping on the Bed*
- Bachelet, Gilles. *My Cat, The Silliest Cat in the World*
- Boynton, Sandra. *Blue Hat, Green Hat*
- Buehner, Carolyn. *It's a Spoon Not a Shovel*
- Child, Lauren. *I Will Never Not Ever Eat a Tomato*
- Cho, Shinta. *The Gas We Pass, The Story of Farts*
- Christelow, Eileen. *Five Little Monkeys Jumping on the Bed*
- Coleman, Michael. *A Silly Snowy Day*
- Cronin, Doreen. *Click Clack Moo*

- Cronin, Doreen. *Diary of a Worm*
- Denim, Sue. *The Dumb Bunnies Go to the Zoo*
- Freiman, Saxton. *How Are You Peeling?*
- Grossman, Bill. *My Little Sister Ate One Hare*
- Gwynne, Fred. *The King Who Rained*
- Hoberman, Mary Ann. *Mary Had a Little Lamb*
- Most, Bernard. *The Cow that Went OINK*
- Numeroff, Laura. *Sometimes I Wonder If Poodles Like Noodles*
- Numeroff, Laura. *If You Give a Mouse a Cookie*
- Palatini, Margie. *The Web Files*
- Parish, Peggy. *Amelia Badelia Collection*
- Rathmann, Peggy. *Goodnight Gorilla*
- Rey, H.A. *Curious George*
- Scieszka, Jon. *The Stinky Cheese Man and Other Fairly Stupid Tales*
- Scieszka, Jon. *The True Story of the Three Little Pigs*
- Shannon, David. *Duck on a Bike*
- Shannon, David. *No David!*
- Slobodkina, Esphyr. *Caps for Sale*
- Small, David. *Imogene's Antlers*
- Stenmark, Victoria. *The Singing Chick*
- Stoeke Morgan, Janet. *Minerva Louise Collection*
- Wood, Audrey. *Silly Sally*
- Websites: www.fotosearch.com, www.amazon.com, and www. biblio.com.

The joy of music

Music is a wonderful and easily accessible activity for engaging a child with autism. There is an abundance of humorous and fun music and musical video/DVDs geared to all age levels. Silly songs can encourage imitation skills (*If You're Happy and You Know It*), imagination (*There Was an Old Lady Who Swallowed a Fly*), and general knowledge (*Old MacDonald*

Had a Farm or *Ten Little Monkeys*). Many videos incorporate music and movement providing additional sensory and cognitive stimulation. Given that individuals with autism require frequent and consistent modeling to acquire skills, it is important to model an appropriate affective response to the visual and verbal cues provided in the music and DVDs, encouraging the children to follow along.

Theme days

Theme days can be a good way to break up a classroom's typical daily routine and inject humor. Possible theme day topics include: silly hats day, wear your pajamas to school day, inside/outside day, crazy hair day, storybook characters day, and animals day. Holidays, current events, and classroom lessons (e.g., learning about community helpers or history stories) can also be used as theme day topics. Whatever the theme, the actions of planning a costume, dressing up, and participating with peers and teachers present many opportunities for playfulness and laughter. Theme days provide a wonderful opportunity for collaboration between parents and teachers when families are asked to help in the planning of their children's theme day costume.

We have discussed how humor can be a potentially beneficial skill for persons with autism. It can foster connections with others and provide a way to cope with tough situations. At the same time, humor is a complex skill that is dependent on a number of cognitive abilities that the person with autism may only partially possess. For this reason, teaching the basic rules about humor and practicing rote responses to humor may be first steps. Because there is such a variety of language, imagination, and cognitive abilities in persons with autism, the activity section begins with more concrete examples. These then become increasingly complex in terms of understanding incongruency and using more advanced language skills.

Chapter 3

Self-Efficacy

Figure 3.1 'I can do it!'

WHAT IS SELF-EFFICACY?

This chapter discusses the importance of self-efficacy. The information presented is aimed at providing the necessary knowledge and skills required to foster self-efficacy in the special needs population, increase abilities to cope effectively with life demands, and improve quality of life.

Self-efficacy is the belief that people have about their ability and readiness to perform a task (Fall and McLeod 2001). For example, you know whether you can get dressed, bake a cake, solve a multiplication problem, fly a space shuttle, or raise a leopard as a pet. The children in Figure 3.1 know that they can be creative in the sandbox. Your appreciation of your capability for each task is your self-efficacy belief (Pajares 2002). To better understand what self-efficacy is, look at the following example.

> Laurie learned to tie her shoe laces, but found this skill challenging. In the beginning, she frequently called others to ask for help and directions. Her self-efficacy for this skill was low, which meant that she did not believe she could tie her shoes on her own. With practice and help, Laurie learned the steps to take to tie her shoes. After a lot of practice and many successes, she acquired high self-efficacy in tying her shoes.

This example describes two important characteristics of self-efficacy. First, Laurie learned that high self-efficacy is based on previous experiences and that she can learn strategies to acquire skills. Individuals with high self-efficacy in a specific task trust in their ability to organize their thoughts and execute courses of action that are needed to manage the challenge (Bandura 1997). Second, self-efficacy can become better appreciated when the individual confronts a task that is challenging.

While self-efficacy is specific in this instance to a shoe-tying task, it can be generalized to refer to different but related activities, such as getting dressed or putting on a shirt (Luszczynska and Gutierrez-Donna 2005).

SELF-EFFICACY AND SELF-ESTEEM

Self-esteem, like self-efficacy, is nurtured by achievements and successes, but self-efficacy is a sense of capability, whereas self-esteem is a sense of self-worth (Pajares 2002). The following example illustrates the difference between the two:

Laurie's mother ties her shoes with ease. She does not feel high self-esteem due to this ability, although her self-efficacy for this task is high. Unlike Mom, tying shoe laces is a source of pride for Laurie. In the beginning, Laurie's self-efficacy in tying shoes was not high, and she called her mother for assistance when she got confused. However, her self-esteem is high, since she is proud of being engaged in learning this challenging skill.

Mastering skills provides an individual with high self-efficacy. At the same time, it nurtures self-esteem only if the individual views his or her self-worth as dependent on this ability.

RATIONALE FOR FOCUSING ON SELF-EFFICACY

Many individuals with autism suffer from learning and emotional challenges that impair their ability to develop self-efficacy (Lewis 1999). Low self-efficacy in turn hampers future learning, by creating vicious cycles of learning resistance, manifested in task avoidance, social avoidances, and fear of challenges and changes. Avoidance of new learning opportunities and engaging in new experiences leads to the loss of opportunities to gain positive self-efficacy beliefs (Brooks 1999; Brooks and Goldstein 2001; Lewis 1999). The impact of low self-efficacy, regrettably, goes beyond the school and particular learning circumstances, and can affect all aspects of an individual's life. Examples of expressions of low self-efficacy in individuals with autism include the following:

- expressed sense of incapability, and expectation of failure
- anxiety response to tasks and demands
- refusal to engage in a new or challenging task
- avoidance behaviors (boredom, sleepiness, feeling sick, forgetfulness, tantrums, reduced attention and eye contact on task) when a task or challenge is presented
- easily lost motivation
- reduced efforts when failing at a task
- negative self-talk about the task, and the associated people and environment
- negative interpretation of outcomes, sensitivity to mistakes
- self-blame.

Self-efficacy affects goal setting

People set their lifelong goals according to their self-efficacy beliefs. These goals are based on their sense of capability to achieve them. Whether we are addressing a student who is considering entering a Special Olympics event, or an individual who is considering which job description fits his or her skills, self-efficacy guides the decisions that are made. Studies show that self-efficacy is even relevant to the choices people make in finding their spouse (Betz and Hackett 1983; Branch and Lichtenberg 1987).

Self-efficacy affects motivation

Students with high self-efficacy in academic subjects expect to succeed. This expectation naturally increases their motivation and effort. Motivation in turn further nurtures students' self-efficacy beliefs. Motivation tends to increase the chance the student has to succeed in an assignment. Motivated students also gain their teachers' appreciation, which supports their self-efficacy beliefs (Alderman 2004).

Students with low self-efficacy are typically unmotivated. They do not expect the reinforcing effect of success, high grade, or appreciative remarks by the teacher. Their low motivation and low efforts, moreover, can be used as an unconscious coping mechanism aimed at protecting their ego from feeling negatively about themselves when they fail. They may feel better about failure if others attribute the reason for their failures to laziness rather than to their inability (Alderman 2004).

Self-efficacy increases persistence

Individuals with high self-efficacy persist in their tasks, and are more resilient to setbacks (Bandura 1993). For example, students with high self-efficacy in math have been found to persist more in their efforts to solve math problems even if those problems are actually unsolvable. On the other hand, individuals with low self-efficacy in math give up earlier in such circumstances (Bandura 1993; Dweck 2000; Schunk and Zimmerman 2007).

High self-efficacy increases hope and optimism

Individuals who have already gained self-efficacy in the presence of a variety of challenges develop a pragmatic attitude toward new challenges, tend to use problem-solving strategies more adeptly, and increase their efforts when the challenge seems especially difficult (Alderman 2004; Dweck 2000).

Low self-efficacy is associated with heightened anxiety levels

People who do not feel ready or capable to perform a task are more anxious when approaching it (Scholz, Dona and Schwarzer 2002). For example, high school students with low self-efficacy in math approach math with more anxiety and utilize fewer problem-solving skills compared to students with higher self-efficacy, when general mental ability is comparable in the groups (Pajares and Kranzler 1995). Especially relevant to our purposes here, individuals with autism tend to suffer from a heightened anxiety response to their expectation of failure (Groden *et al.* 1994). Increasing self-efficacy in relation to daily stressors can potentially help such individuals become less provoked by these challenges.

THE DEVELOPMENT OF SELF-EFFICACY

Self-efficacy beliefs are developed by having empowering experiences that lead individuals to trust their own capabilities. The noted psychologist Albert Bandura (1997) recognized and wrote about sources of information that are required to develop self-efficacy beliefs. These include the following:

- learning about one's capabilities through experience (mastery experiences)
- comparing oneself to others (vicarious learning)
- experiencing the body's physiological response to the challenge
- assimilating and adopting others' beliefs about one's capability (persuasion).

Further, studies have provided insights into how the interpretation and judgment of outcomes is processed by individuals to provide them with self-efficacy.

Learning about one's capabilities through experience (mastery experiences)

Experiences that are interpreted as successful tend to increase self-efficacy, while experiences that are interpreted as failures reduce it, as shown in the following example:

> Nicole, who is an excellent student in math, feels more self-efficacious when she receives another A grade on her most recent test. A C grade may reduce her self-efficacy. The effect of an experience on one's self-efficacy is greater if it comes before any sense of efficacy in this area has been established. For example, the C grade does not affect Nicole's self-efficacy to a great extent if she has experienced many A's before that test in the same subject, and with the same teacher. It would be tougher on her if she received a C on the first exam in a new subject or with a new teacher.

A strong sense of self-efficacy can therefore buffer the effect of random failures.

Students with learning disabilities often suffer from repeated experiences of failures. Early success in a given task can increase the individual's self-efficacy and can foster immunity from occasional failures. It is important to teach in a way that provides the greatest possibility to gain success early in the process.

Comparing oneself to others (vicarious learning)

Vicarious or observational learning refers to a process of acquiring knowledge or a skill by watching a model (another person) perform a skill or a targeted task. The impact of modeling on self-efficacy is strongly influenced by the similarity of the model to the observer. For example, a child watching a peer who is learning tennis will have better results than watching a professional tennis player.

The effect of vicarious learning on self-efficacy in individuals with autism has hardly been studied at all. However, modeling was found to be an effective tool in teaching children with autism to perform different skills such as playing with toys, following class routines, and focusing on activities (Carden Smith and Fowler 1984; Fowler 1986). Vicarious learning may be effective in developing self-efficacy in students with autism, and in reducing the anxiety associated with engaging in challenging tasks. For example, some students who have autism learn photography as part of their art curriculum. Students who would like to use the camera become less apprehensive when they join peers who volunteer to try first (Kantor and Groden 2007). Vicarious learning reduces their anxiety and allows them to develop positive self-efficacy beliefs that help them to engage in the activity.

Video modeling is a promising strategy that is used in teaching individuals with autism. This method is found to be equal to or more effective than *in-vivo* modeling (Bellini and Akullian 2007; Charlop, Schreibman and Tyron 1983; Charlop-Christy and Daneshvar 2003). It involves a child watching a videotape that captures the child (self-modeling) or similar others performing a desired behavior. In self-modeling, students watch a videotape of themselves performing an activity that they do well. The advantages of video modeling to the learner with autism are as follows:

- The videos are produced so that they are focused on the relevant cues.

- Watching videos is fun and reinforcing for many individuals with autism.

- Watching modeling through videos requires less social interaction than viewing a real-life model.

Experiencing the body's physiological response to the challenge

Physiological and affective states such as anxiety, stress, excitement, and mood also provide information about efficacy beliefs. People tend to focus on their physiological reactions as a source of self-efficacy information. Individuals who tend to become anxious when engaging in a task may feel less self-efficacious. On the other hand, if individuals experience elation when confronted with a challenging task, their self-efficacy increases. Individuals with autism are more sensitive and overreact to minor environmental stimulation such as noise, light, and crowds.

Assimilating and adopting others' beliefs about one's capability (persuasion)

We all use persuasion as a common strategy for convincing someone to engage in a challenging task. People may say, 'You did it before, so of course you can do it again!' or, 'If Sarah did it, you can definitely do it!' or, 'Take a deep breath, relax, and make this phone call!' Persuasions are the verbal statements that people make when they encourage another person to engage in a challenging task, compare that person's abilities favorably to others, and help control a person's physiological reactions to stress. In their statements, the persuaders encourage the development of positive attributions.

Persuasion is considered by Bandura (1997) to be the least effective method to affect self-efficacy beliefs. However, Segal (1988) says the importance of persuasion and encouragement that is provided constantly by a parent, a teacher, or peers, can have a very strong empowering and persuading effect on a child. In any form of encouragement and persuasion, the child must perceive the persuader as credible, and the persuasive statements must focus on reasonable and achievable goals.

Expressed expectations are also sources of information about self-efficacy, and can be considered as persuasions, as long as the expectations are realistic. Low expectations are often communicated indirectly and inadvertently, such as when teachers offer sympathy rather than constructive feedback, or praise excessively for trivial achievements, or provide support when it is not required. Even assigning students to groups based on low academic capabilities can be detrimental to self-efficacy (Alderman 2004; Bracke, Christiaens and Verhaeghe 2008; Lewis 1999).

INTERPRETATION AND JUDGMENT OF OUTCOMES

Individuals judge their capabilities based on their cognitive beliefs and attributional style which can greatly affect the development of self-efficacy, as described in the following example:

> Jenny, age 11, gets stressed when she struggles with a reading comprehension assignment. She looks around and figures that she is slower than most of the students, and concludes that she is dumb. Aaron, whose skills levels are comparable to those of Jenny, works on his assignment, too. He struggles, but uses some strategies that he has practiced, and asks for more time to finish his assignment. As a result, he is satisfied with the progress of his work.

Jenny and Aaron are very different in their judgment of their achievements. Their differences can be explained from several perspectives, as illustrated below.

Measuring one's own progress

Jenny judges her self-efficacy by comparing herself to the brighter students in her class. She assumes their real or imaginary abilities as the desired goal. Her focus is on the immediate results; either she has the skills or she is stupid. Aaron, on the other hand, feels successful with his progress and judges his achievements without comparison to others. He can envision how his efforts will eventually lead him to his goals (Alderman 2004).

Emotional sensitivity

Many people have high and sometimes unrealistic self-expectations. However, some people take disappointments more gracefully than others. People who suffer tremendously when their expectations are not met are regarded as perfectionists who typically respond with tremendous pain, self-criticism, and self-deprecation (Frost *et al.* 1990). These characteristics compromise self-efficacy beliefs. Jenny may suffer from perfectionism and be prone to depression, anxiety, hostility, and anger. She probably engages in increased rumination over failures. Perfectionists view assignments as a threat, assign higher importance to assignments than other students, and view a failure as a catastrophe. They do not enjoy challenges, and are more worried about being judged as in some way deficient by others (Besser, Flett and Hewitt 2004).

Students may develop perfectionism on their own. However, parents and teachers can also lead a child to develop *socially prescribed* perfectionism by setting unrealistic expectations. The child may be motivated in some instances by the need for approval from others rather than the academic interest (Hewitt and Flett 1991).

Negative attributions about accomplishments

Jenny's style of attribution tends to be personal, stable, and global (Seligman *et al.* 1995). She believes that her difficulty in reading is caused by being dumb (personal attribution), and may also believe that it affects all of her school achievements (global attribution) and that it cannot be changed (stable attribution). Holding constant negative self-beliefs about her intelligence may become a major obstacle for developing self-efficacy, and may contribute to future failures. These beliefs may lead to expressions of indifference or laziness toward academic demands. These behaviors can be motivated by a need to avoid frustration and pain related to the task. For students with high social awareness, expressions of indifference may come from a need to protect one's self-image. Such students would rather attribute their failures to a lack of effort than a lack of ability (Alderman 2004).

Studies that focus on developing self-efficacy suggest several approaches that may benefit individuals who tend to judge themselves harshly. Such approaches include developing realistic expectations of the learning process, focusing on short-term personally tailored goals, improving learning skills, and setting a positive learning atmosphere that focuses on effort and cooperation.

NURTURING SELF-EFFICACY IN INDIVIDUALS WITH AUTISM

Individuals approach tasks with high self-efficacy if they previously learned strategies that allow them to plan their action, and if they believe in their abilities to put these strategies into action. Parents and teachers can help students develop a positive learning environment and increase the likelihood of establishing a track record of success by implementing principles and strategies such as those stated below.

Teaching effectively

Learning and feeling good about using skills are the key elements in nurturing self-efficacy. Many individuals, including those with autism, benefit greatly from discrete trial training, errorless learning, and task analysis strategies, when learning challenging academic, daily life, and vocational skills. These methods break skills down into small manageable steps, and reduce errors and frustration. Learning skills successfully is the first step in acquiring self-efficacy. Some of the lesson plans in the area of self-efficacy demonstrate how these methods can be applied to benefit individuals with intense learning needs.

Focusing on skills that increase self-efficacy

Learners should be encouraged to increase their self-management and executive-skills strategies to enhance their coping, using such tasks as the following:

- breaking down tasks into small manageable steps
- using lists, journals, and daily schedules to remember tasks
- practicing coping skills for stressful events
- staying on task, overcoming distractions
- gathering, learning, and sorting relevant information related to a task or a challenge
- prioritizing tasks
- avoiding procrastination.

Reinforcing controllable components

While many typically developing students are frequently intrinsically reinforced by experiencing their success, students with disabilities often struggle with failures, and therefore are more dependent on others to provide extrinsic reinforcers to keep them motivated. In inclusive classrooms, their difficulties and struggles may become more apparent to them, threatening their positive self-efficacy beliefs. When watching how others are reinforced for their talents, students who do not consider themselves talented may feel hopeless (Reis and Colbert 2004). Self-efficacy beliefs can be reinforced for these students by stressing the importance of controllable elements that affect achievements (Alderman 2004). Examples of controllable elements that can be reinforced include effort, motivation, self-control, determination, responsibility, discipline, cooperation, time management, and application of the skills learned. Increased executive and problem-solving skills will eventually lead to increased self-efficacy.

Providing positive attributions

Students can state the following realistic and positive beliefs as alternatives to negative thinking:

- My learning, my grades, and even my intelligence can be improved, by studying.

- When I am overwhelmed by tasks I should stop (relax), get organized (make a list, set priorities, set a schedule), and then act (get to work)!
- I can't expect myself to know something if I have never learned it before.
- It takes a lot of time and effort to really understand some of the materials!
- Learning and practicing will make a difference.
- It's alright to make mistakes! Everybody does!
- No one is good at everything.
- Each of us has talents in different areas.
- I am not expected to be perfect! Nobody is perfect!
- It is important for me to do my personal best.
- I can contribute even if I am not the very best.

Nurturing self-management skills

Self-management skills are found to expedite the acquisition of academic, play, and social skills (Lee, Simpson and Shogren 2007; Morrison *et al.* 2001). Self-management skills reduce impulsivity, increase self-monitoring skills, and foster independence in individuals with autism (Newman, Reinecke and Meinberg 2000; Stahmer and Schreibman 1992). Students with autism can learn self-management by discrete teaching of the skills needed to evaluate their own and others' behaviors, and then practicing and applying these skills in various settings while fading the materials. Participation in the monitoring of self and others increases self-management skills and insights toward one's own behaviors, and their impact on others.

SELF-MONITORING

Self-monitoring is defined as the ability to observe and determine one's own behavior (Morrison *et al.* 2001). In general, students tend to report about 50 percent of their incorrect behaviors or incidents, and become better reporters with the improvement of their skills (Stahmer and Schreibman 1992). Examples of different recording techniques include using a chronograph alarm wristwatch or filling out a chart using pencils or stickers. Students can also independently collect a token for each correct response (Newman *et al.* 2000). Students can progress by increasing the time intervals in which self-monitoring is recorded. Students can also be provided with charts to monitor chores that class teams are assigned, such as cleaning up specific areas in the classroom, or doing study assignments without being disruptive, to increase their awareness of the desired behaviors (Carden Smith and Fowler 1984).

SELF-EVALUATING

Students learn to compare their behaviors to standard behaviors or goals (Morrison *et al.* 2001). The students summarize their behavior by documenting it on a form. The form can consist of a set of questions such as, 'Did you finish your homework?' or a graph which charts the amount of tokens received (Stahmer and Schreibman 1992).

INVOLVING STUDENTS IN GOAL SETTING

Students who set their educational and behavioral goals, such as how many pages they will read a day, how many towels they will fold during their chore time, or how many math problems they will solve in their scheduled math time, are more motivated to reach their goals than students whose goals are dictated to them (Schunk 1985). Students with autism usually need more support and direction in setting goals, especially if they lack a sense of measure of time, or if it will take an understanding of the complexity of their goal. In such instances, teachers can provide a reasonable goal range for the student to choose from, such as setting a goal with a range between two and five pages.

CONCLUSION

Self-efficacy is developed by cumulative successful learning experiences. Individuals with autism who often struggle with learning new skills are exposed to frequent experiences of failure. Teaching skills, nurturing controllable positive behaviors and habits that lead to productivity, and increasing the learners' awareness of their capabilities can benefit their self-efficacy. Attending to factors in the environment, reviewing expectations and behaviors of parents and teachers, choosing effective teaching methods, increasing self-management and coping skills, and helping individuals to *own* their success can all increase self-efficacy in individuals with autism.

Chapter 4

Kindness

Figure 4.1 Considering the needs of others is an important component of kindness

WHAT IS KINDNESS?

Aristotle described kindness as 'helpfulness towards someone in need, not in return for anything, nor for the advantage of the helper himself, but for that of the person helped' (Ross 2010, p.150).

Through the ages, kindness has been understood to be engagement in acts which may be characterized as warm-hearted, considerate, humane, sympathetic, and forgiving. Describing someone as warm-hearted means the person is seen as doing things which demonstrate the person's desire to help others. Being considerate involves behaving in a way that prioritizes the needs of others above one's own. Being humane involves acts which are gentle and benevolent in nature. Sympathy connotes actions which demonstrate an ability to empathize with and validate the emotional needs of another. Forgiveness involves demonstrating that another person is not considered to be indebted to the forgiving person.

When a person's outward behavior is consistent with these attributes, we deem the individual to be kind. Kind people, when presented with an opportunity, make choices to do thoughtful and benevolent things for others. They are able to shift their focus of awareness and understanding from self to others and respond with deeds and actions that are informed by these sensitivities. In Figure 4.1, the older child considers the needs of the younger child, and kindly gives her a pumpkin. In this chapter, we discuss theories of kindness and offer a rationale for teaching and fostering kindness in children with autism and other developmental disorders.

RATIONALE FOR FOCUSING ON KINDNESS

Researching kindness and autism often focuses on treating individuals with autism with kindness. Attention to the caretaker's or teacher's attitude and behavior in relation to the student is the obvious initial perspective. But what of the reverse perspective? How do we teach individuals with autism and developmental disabilities to be kind, altruistic, and helpful toward others? Consider the following benefits of being kind:

- Kindness is sustained by positive feedback from the environment. Kind acts are, by nature, positive social interactions that benefit others and provide the giver with a sense of personal satisfaction and self-esteem in having done the right thing (see Figure 4.2).

- Kindness pays back socially as well. Acting kindly means an individual is able to expand one's focus of interest beyond oneself. For example, kind individuals are typically well liked by their peers. They have developed an empathetic understanding which is the affective and cognitive ability to understand and share another's feelings and perspective.

- Kind behavior requires the student to employ valuable social, coping, and problem-solving skills and makes the individual more insightful and resourceful. When we encourage students to act kindly toward others, we promote both the recipient and the giver's self-esteem and sense of well-being.

- Research has demonstrated a positive correlation between students' training and skills in empathetic understanding and their academic performance (Cotton 2001).

- Kindness is associated with good learning. It has been demonstrated that individuals who self-monitor acts of kindness have increased scores on scales measuring happiness. They report having more happy memories (Lyubomirsky and Lepper 1999; Otake *et al.* 2006).

- If persons with disabilities can be taught to administer kind acts, they will more likely be accepted as contributors in their communities. Teaching kindness provides them with the opportunity to give back to others and to the larger community, and to step out of their more familiar, dependent roles as consumers of services.

Although students with developmental disabilities are often challenged to comprehend empathy and other emotional and social skills that are embedded in kind behavior, it *is possible* to teach kind deeds and other prosocial behavior related to kindness.

In a special education setting, kindness can be a vehicle for students to participate in reciprocal relationships with others. If students are volunteering or helping in the larger community, they are participating in reciprocal relationships with community members and creating more social, educational, and vocational opportunities for themselves and for others. Treating others with kindness increases the likelihood that others will respond positively and that relationships within the school and community will be enhanced. This is best illustrated by what can be considered a positive feedback loop whereby the performer is reinforced for kindness which then leads to further positive interactions. Figure 4.2 shows this schematically.

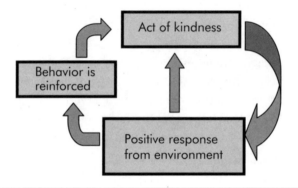

Figure 4.2 Kind behavior is reinforced by the positive response from the environment, leading to an increase in kind behavior

COMPONENTS OF KINDNESS: EMPATHY AND PERSPECTIVE TAKING

The ability to perceive the emotional needs of another is called empathy. Cotton (2001) asserts that a proper education includes 'insight into motives, feelings, and behaviors of others and the ability to communicate this understanding – in a word, empathy.' McCollough (1992) echoed this sentiment in this way: 'Moral imagination is the capacity to empathize with others, i.e., not just to feel for oneself, but to feel with and for others.' Empathy requires perspective taking, or the ability to perceive and/or understand the world from another's point of view (Selman 1971).

Perspective taking (PT) is a prosocial skill that requires social awareness, or the ability to infer the capabilities, attributes, expectations, feelings, and potential reactions of others. PT plays an important part in social problem solving, communication and persuasion, understanding fairness and justice (Selman 1975), and moral reasoning (Ambron and Irwin 1975; Selman 1971). Seeing the world from another's point of view may, in and of itself, not be a kind act but allows one to assess a situation that may set the stage for behavior that is judged to be altruistically motivated (Krebs and Russell 1981). Selman (1980) describes developmental levels of PT illustrated in Table 4.1.

Table 4.1 The development of perspective taking (adapted from Selman 1980)

Ages	Level	Description
3–6	Egocentric PT	Has a sense of self–other differentiation but not perspectives, thoughts, or feelings
5–9	Social–informational PT	Is aware that perspectives are similar or different, but perspectives are still unrelated
7–12	Self-reflective PT	Reflects on own emotions and cognitions and anticipates others'. Cannot abstract to simultaneous mutuality
10–15	Mutual PT	Can view two-person (i.e., self–other) interaction from a third-person perspective. Understands both self and others. Can view each other mutually and simultaneously
15 and up	Social and conventional systematic PT	Perspectives are part of and influenced by social and conventional systems. Understood as necessary because they belong to all members of the group

HOW IS KINDNESS NURTURED IN TYPICAL CHILDREN?

Empathy may be seen as a vital skill in producing a kind act (Cotton 2001; McCollough 1992), and is part of a child's learning experience even before entering school. Research indicates that mothers who are responsive and not overly punitive or authoritarian toward their children are more likely to raise children who exhibit prosocial behavior (Eisenberg, Lennon and Roth 1983; Elicker, Englund and Sroufe 1992; Zahn-Waxler, Radke-Yarrow and King 1979). Also, reasoning with children, even those who are quite young, about the effects of their behavior on others and the importance of sharing and being kind is effective in promoting empathy and prosocial behavior (Clarke 1984; Ladd, Lange and Stremmel 1983; Zahn-Waxler *et al.* 1979).

Throughout children's preschool life, parental interaction helps mold their understanding of what is appropriate or not. At a child's very early age, many parents respond to selfishness with disapproval, while positively reinforcing sharing. They also model empathetic and caring behavior by the way they interact with their children. These empathetic interactions strongly influence the attitudes and behaviors developed by the child

(Eisenberg-Berg and Mussen 1978; Zahn-Waxler *et al.* 1979). Conversely, when children hurt others or otherwise cause them distress, research supports the idea that the practice of giving explanations as to why the behaviors are harmful and giving suggestions for how to make amends can also play a significant role in changing such inappropriate behavior (Zahn-Waxler *et al.* 1979).

As children grow older, they often have more structured opportunities to develop empathetic skills and to be rewarded for acts of kindness. Playing games that require social interaction encourages the child to take another's point of view. Activities that require individuals to assume the role of a real or fictional person, and to imagine or act out that person's behavior, have been shown to facilitate both affective and cognitive empathy (Barak *et al.* 1987; Black and Phillips 1982; Herbek and Yammarino 1990; Kremer and Dietzen 1991; Morgan 1983; Underwood and Moore 1982). The child's role-playing gains greater effectiveness with ongoing use. Further, researchers have shown that it is necessary to have repeated practice in learning to take another person's perspective (Black and Phillips 1982; Kremer and Dietzen 1991; Pecukonis 1990). Another effective element in a child's learning of empathy and kindness is exposure to emotionally arousing stimuli. Exposure to portrayals of misfortune, deprivation, or distress on the part of others tends to increase the chances of an empathetic response (Barnett *et al.* 1982; Howard and Barnett 1981; Pecukonis 1990; Perry, Bussey and Freiberg 1981).

KINDNESS IN AUTISM

If performing acts of kindness requires the ability to empathize with others and engage in PT, then being kind presents an immediate difficulty for persons with autism. In order to act kindly one must perceive social cues that indicate the needs and current emotional states of another. By definition, autism is a disorder that involves deficits in social awareness. Therefore, people with autism have difficulty identifying, understanding, and appropriately reacting to the social and emotional needs of others. Further, persons with autism may miss the opportunity to learn kindness through modeling which is an important method for learning kindness (Eisenberg *et al.* 1983; Eisenberg-Berg and Mussen 1978; Kestenbaum, Farber and Sroufe 1989; Zahn-Waxler *et al.* 1979). Kindness is often triggered by a sense of reciprocity (essentially the principle of 'one good turn deserves another'). Individuals with autism do not find it easy to learn reciprocity and, therefore, most often do not participate in the exchange of kind acts.

Another reason why individuals with autism have limited experiences as providers of needs is that society, more often than not, does not view them in this way. Many persons with autism are often the recipients of multiple supports and services and are therefore more likely to have experiences as consumers rather than providers. Many people and programs tend to view individuals with disabilities as less accountable for unkind acts. Since people tend to like those who help them and develop reciprocal relationships with them, practicing kind acts can be a very effective way for people with autism to change this type of thinking and develop meaningful relationships. They can be seen in this way not only as consumers and dependents in their community but also as contributors and givers.

TEACHING KINDNESS TO INDIVIDUALS WITH AUTISM

Various innovative methods have been implemented as a means to teach individuals with autism to develop a sense of empathy and to engage in acts of kindness. Here are some examples.

Picture rehearsal

The picture rehearsal approach involves presenting various scripts to the student that promote the performance of kind deeds.

Drama and role-playing

Role-play of kind deeds in the classroom can be used to practice kind behaviors. Teachers can reinforce the role play of opening doors, picking up an item that someone drops, helping people to carry heavy shopping bags, and so on. Since students play both the performer of kind acts as well as the recipient of the deed, they experience both the emotional satisfaction of being kind and being on the receiving end of the kindness. The use of video modeling, in which role-play scenarios are taped and then played back to students, gives the students visual feedback on their performance of benevolent behavior.

Animal therapy

Animal therapy helps develop empathy and kindness toward other living things and can be an intrinsically rewarding experience. The goal of this program is to expose participants to animals that require kindness and caring, modeling such behavior, and then naming the behavior as kindness for the student. Children are encouraged to engage with an animal (often a dog) in a variety of ways. An engagement could take place as follows: the animal therapist and other staff seat the students about ten feet away from the dog, or behind their desk or a table. Each student in turn picks one *choice card* such as petting or feeding the dog. The teacher labels the kind act performed by the child. For example, when the student gives a dog a treat, the teacher says, 'You gave the dog a treat. You are very kind to the dog. The dog loves to get treats.' When the student brushes a dog, the teacher says, 'It's very kind of you to brush the dog. It makes the dog very happy to be brushed.' When engaging with the animal, the student should be given positive feedback.

Kind deeds program

Throughout the course of a school day, students are encouraged to perform kind acts both in planned and incidental teaching situations. In order to increase the generalization and the spontaneity of kind acts, students can also learn to look for helping opportunities. Some examples include:

- holding doors for others
- assisting the teacher or a peer in carrying something
- bringing a needed item (e.g., napkin, pen, or book) to someone
- sharing classroom materials
- sharing a personal item or food
- contributing to a group effort (e.g., setting out napkins for a snack)
- cooperating with teacher requests to help with classroom tasks (e.g., errands to the office)
- helping teachers and peers who require assistance
- feeding fish or watering plants
- complimenting other students and teachers.

Positive affirmations

In this program, a list is constructed with the student which includes kind acts that the student has demonstrated and used. The student then reads these on a daily basis. For example, one item might be 'I am a kind person, I like to help others.'

Volunteering in the community

Encouraging and rewarding acts of kindness are also an important component of community-based vocational services. While the purpose of these programs is to immerse the students with autism in their community while teaching them communication and vocational skills, these volunteer programs have a major kindness component.

The Meals on Wheels program uses volunteers to make daily meal delivery to indigent and housebound elderly people and individuals with disabilities. This program is founded on the premise of service and kind acts. While engaging in their Meals on Wheels deliveries, students perform multiple kind acts ranging from the actual meal delivery to holding doors for others, carrying coolers for the group, and engaging in social interactions with meal recipients. The staff support the students in carrying out these acts by providing appropriate verbal and tangible reinforcement. Emphasis on kind acts that serve needy community members is important. Engaging in these tasks emphasizes the responsibility of students as members of a cooperative society.

The Groden Network's adult program, the Cove Center, also systematically teaches the individuals it supports the value of kind deeds. The Kindness Tree program provides instruction to its participants by a variety of methods during structured sessions. Staff members observe participants and record acts of kindness that they display throughout the day. Participants are then encouraged to document their observed acts on paper leaves and place the leaves on the Kindness Tree, which is displayed in the main lobby. Participants feel a sense of accomplishment as they watch the tree burst into leaf.

The Kind Deed Recognition Program at the Cove Center is another important component of the Center's curriculum that helps to promote kindness on the part of the people it supports. The goals of this program are for its participants to have the positive experience of performing kind deeds, and receiving positive feedback from others. Clients are given a choice of kindness activities; some individuals require direct instruction (e.g., 'It's time to do this now') and are given a tangible reward coupled with immediate praise for performing a kind deed. Other more independent individuals receive few or no prompts and several choices of kind deeds to perform, and then perhaps take part in a discussion of what they did and why it was kind. All participants receive kind deed cards from staff as a reward. These cards are posted for public recognition and/or are exchanged for a tangible reward.

CONCLUSION

The poet and novelist Kahlil Gibran (1997) wrote, 'You give but little when you give of your possessions. It is when you give of yourself that you truly give' (p.17). Individuals with autism, however, have difficulties perceiving social cues which should indicate the needs of others and prompt an act of kindness. These difficulties are not insurmountable. It is possible to help individuals learn how to give of themselves. This type of behavior is an important building block for individuals to become contributors to the community in which they live.

THE HOPE STREET BEAUTIFICATION PROJECT

The Hope Street Beautification Project is part of a cooperative effort with the city of Providence to beautify its neighborhoods. The students range in age from 11 to 21 and have various levels of skills and abilities. During the winter and early spring the project takes place in a greenhouse operated by the Groden Center. At the greenhouse students learn about soil, fertilizer, and seeds; prepare planting beds; and plant and care for the flowers. In May, the Groden Center students transplant the flowers into large planters which are positioned along a section of Hope Street in Providence, as shown in Figure 4.3. The planters extend for a quarter of a mile in a section of the city comprised mainly of small shops, restaurants, and other businesses. Students maintain these planters by watering and

---

weeding them several times a week. This affords the students opportunities to enjoy, and thereby be reinforced for, the care of living things.

Working at this location also gives the students occasion to interact with the merchants and residents of the Hope Street area. During interactions with other community members, students receive positive feedback for appropriate social skills that enhance community involvement and the development of meaningful relationships. As these positive interactions progress, the students learn through natural contingencies the likes and dislikes of others and how to respond to both. This understanding is the seed for further development of social skills that can be generalized to other settings. Students are thereby able to practice socialization skills on a first-hand basis within a community context and view social interactions as rewarding experiences.

Figure 4.3 Students of the Groden Center take care of plants on Hope Street, Providence

Chapter 5

Resilience

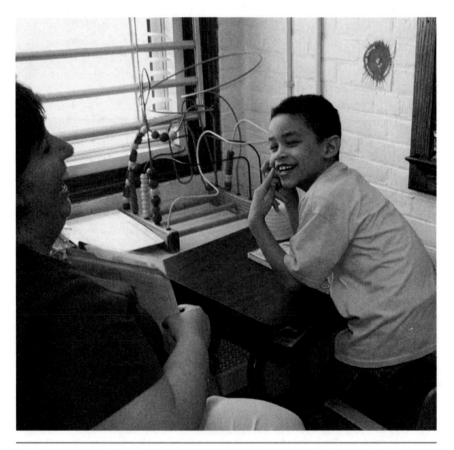

Figure 5.1 Students at the Groden Center are encouraged to make 'trying again' fun

WHAT IS RESILIENCE?

For individuals with autism and developmental disabilities, the development of resilience may be compromised due to deficits in emotional and social competencies. To nurture resilience, we should first understand what resilience is, how resilience develops, and what fosters or impedes its development. Due to the scarce amount of research related to resilience in autism, we can only draw upon studies of typically developing children and youth to discover ways to address the unique experiences and needs of individuals with autism.

Understanding childhood as a life-defining period brought attention to children who live under severe adversities, such as in war zones or in extreme poverty. Scientists who attempted to find strategies to help these children noticed that the psychological development of some is less harmed than others. Curiosity to figure out the protective mechanisms that shield these children from harm initiated the study of resilience.

The concept of resilience and its role in helping individuals thrive is of inestimable importance especially in the population of individuals with autism. We speak of resilient individuals as those who persevere, carry on, and triumph over challenges and adversity. Figure 5.1 shows a student continuing to work despite his challenging program.

Ann Masten defines resilience as 'The process of, capacity for, or outcome of, successful adaptation despite challenging or threatening circumstances' (Masten, Best and Garmezy 1990, p.425). Brooks and Goldstein (2001), in their book on *Raising Resilient Children*, offer this definition:

> Resilience is the capacity to cope and feel competent. The resilient child deals more effectively with stress and pressure, responds effectively to challenges, 'bounces back' from adversity and trauma, and develops clear and realistic goals. This child would also deal better with social situations and enjoy more social acceptance. (Brooks and Goldstein 2001, p.1)

Resilient children cope effectively when faced with threat, stress, hardship, and obstructions. The impact of adversities on their psychological well-being and overall development is less debilitating. Resilience can be viewed as an emotional or psychological shield that protects one from the damaging effects of life's more negative elements.

RATIONALE FOR FOCUSING ON RESILIENCE

Resilience is expressed as pragmatic and effective approaches to difficulties. Resilient individuals are better able to deal effectively with frustrations and worries, and they are able to stay focused on their academic goals. People who are less resilient tend to become more upset, worried, avoidant, or aggressive when challenged, and feel defeated even before making an effort (Alderman 2004). They may also exhibit unsuccessful adaptation that leads to later consequences such as dropping out of school, inability to hold stable jobs, and difficulty in forming stable intimate and familial relationships (Masten *et al.* 1990). More acute manifestations are criminal involvement, drug addiction, and violence. In individuals with autism and developmental disabilities, lack of resilience may impact daily functioning, severity of pathology, and even the overall quality of life.

The following are examples of emotional resilience that affect social and academic functioning (adapted from Bernard 2004). Persons who are emotionally resilient:

- react to challenges with proactive approaches (asking for help from a teacher, parent, or a friend) rather than using avoidance as a coping mechanism (forgetting to do homework, pretending to be sick)

- have a constructive attitude and do not get overly embarrassed and self-deprecative when making mistakes

- avoid blaming others or becoming overly frustrated or angry when disappointed

- do not become self-depreciative when peers seem to understand their schoolwork and do better on tests

- remain calm before important tests, events, or performing in public

- do not worry about popularity with peers

- can cope appropriately when peers are mean, tease, or ignore them.

Persons with autism and developmental disabilities have unique challenges that make them vulnerable in the face of adversity. Their ability to cope and adjust is dependent upon their cognitive capabilities, communication skills, flexibility, and social problem-solving capacities, which often are limited. Deficits in coping skills constitute significant contributing factors to an increased vulnerability, which can lead to anxiety and depression often seen in individuals with autism (Bailey *et al.* 2000; Baron *et al.* 2006; Butzer and Konstantareas 2003; Costello and Angold 1995; Groden *et al.* 1994; Groden *et al.* 2001; Muris *et al.* 1998).

FACTORS THAT MAKE PERSONS WITH AUTISM MORE VULNERABLE AND LESS RESILIENT

The following factors make individuals with autism more vulnerable and less resilient:

- Exaggerated physiological response to challenges: excessive sweating and hormone secretion, and increased heart rate, blood pressure and skin temperature (Goodwin *et al.* 2006; Romanczyk and Gillis 2006).

- Increased anxiety over what most would consider simple daily activities, such as going on a bus ride, a change in routine, or entering a public place (Groden *et al.* 2001; Romanczyk and Gillis 2006).

- Limited repertoire of coping skills and problem-solving skills due to learning disabilities, compromised cognition, communication, and social skills.

- Social interactions are a potential source of stress and anxiety rather than a source of joy and support (Bauminger, Shulman and Agam 2004; Lewis 1999).

- Limited ability to access social support at a time of crisis due to social isolation and communication impairments (Bauminger *et al.* 2004; Bellini 2004).

- Frequent experiences of failures in school and extracurricular activities (Lewis 1999).

- Lack of encouragement of autonomy by teachers and caregivers (Clark *et al.* 2004). As a result, individuals with special needs may develop an increased sense of helplessness and hopelessness (Brown *et al.* 1993; Clark *et al.* 2004).

- Exceptionally high levels of stress and tension, and the high divorce rate among families who have a child with autism challenges the availability of the family to act as a support system (Bouma and Schweitzer 1990; Klauber 1998).

- Individuals with high-functioning autism can experience profound emotional pain as a result of their awareness of the impact of their disability on their lives (Barnhill and Myles 2001; Bauminger *et al.* 2004; Bellini 2004; Garber and Flynn 2001; Kim *et al.* 2000).

WHAT CAN BE DONE TO FOSTER RESILIENCE?

As with typically developing persons, fostering resilience in individuals with autism may assist them in dealing more effectively with their stresses and adversity, which in turn will support emotional stability, and perhaps advance their social and academic development. More specifically, nurturing resilience can help students with autism and special needs to become:

- capable of reacting more adaptively to everyday demands and stressors
- capable of using self-control and positive strategies as alternative means of handling frustration and anger
- more socially and emotionally connected by demonstrating increased tolerance and affection toward others and by taking pleasure in social interactions and responses
- motivated to put effort and interest into achievement and learning
- more open to trying new things and having diverse experiences
- more aware of, and able to express their needs to the best of their abilities
- advocates for themselves and their hopes and aspirations
- problem solvers who seek help when they need it and/or are ready to accept help when it is offered
- more willing to try again even in the face of failure
- recognized for their abilities rather than for their disabilities.

NURTURING RESILIENCE

Resilience is referred to as an 'ordinary magic' since it develops and is stimulated naturally if circumstances allow it (Masten 2001). However, different factors may hamper its development in some children, harming their ability to cope effectively with challenges. Studies of resilience reveal factors that affect its development. The results of the studies described here provide a framework for an intervention specifically for individuals with developmental challenges.

Parents and professionals are often aware of the physical, emotional, intellectual, and social development of children, but less noticed is the development of the adaptation system. The human adaptation system is a set of psychological skills and resources used by individuals when faced with stress and adversity (Masten 2001; Yates and Masten 2004). Successful outcomes lead us to characterize the individual as resilient.

The factors that affect the adaptation system and resilience are either internal (personal qualities and skills) or external (within the environment, e.g., school, family, and peers). Factors that can support resilience (skills, capabilities, resources, and experiences) are defined as protective factors, and those that challenge the adaptation system and resilience are defined as risk factors (Masten and Coatsworth 1998; Masten and Reed 2002; Masten *et al.* 1990). The same source that provides protection of emotional well-being to one person can be a risk factor for another. The balance between the support provided by the protective factors and the burden of the risk factors determines the ability of an individual to overcome adversity successfully.

INTERNAL (PERSONAL) FACTORS

Resilient individuals are characterized as having low levels of distress and emotionality, easy temperament, and average or above average cognitive skills (Bauman 2002; Werner 2000). A review of the literature suggests that resilient children possess the strengths of social competence, autonomy, and problem-solving skills, with a sense of purpose and care about the future (Bauman 2002). The qualities that support these strengths are summarized in Table 5.1.

Table 5.1 Characteristics of the resilient child (adapted from Bauman 2002)

Social competence	Sense of autonomy
• Responsiveness and retrieval of positive responses from the environment • Flexibility • Empathy and caring • Good communicative skills • Developed sense of humor • Ability to recognize and use resources for support during adversity and crisis	• Sense of identity • Independence • Control over the environment • Sense of task mastery • Internal locus of control • Detachment from dysfunctional family, peers, and situations • Resistance to negative messages about self from others • Self-efficacy
Sense of purpose and future	**Problem-solving skills**
• Healthy expectations • Goal directedness • Educational aspiration • High motivation to achieve • Persistence • Hardiness • Optimism and hopefulness • Anticipation for the future	• Developed abstract thinking • Flexibility • Ability to reflect • Attempting different solutions to cognitive and social problems

Resilient individuals use these skills and capabilities when facing adversity, navigating their way through difficulties by negotiating, inventing solutions, recognizing and creating resources, and attracting social support.

EXTERNAL FACTORS

Family, school, and peers were found to contribute to the development of resilience in children by nurturing their attachment, and the 'pleasure in mastery adaptation system' (Masten and Coatsworth 1998; for further details see page 82).

Attachment

The social atmosphere around a person plays a critical role in nurturing resiliency if it provides strong early bonding, positive social support, and later, modeling of effective coping. Individuals nurture a person's adaptation system simply by demonstrating effective problem-solving strategies, by providing good advice and guidance, and by supporting the individual emotionally at times of crisis. Good role models also express their belief in the person's worth and capability, which in turn encourages one to develop positive self-concept. The notion that it takes a village to raise a child is very appropriate when considering the nurturance of resilience, since modeling and support can be provided to children not only by caregivers, but also by other family members, favorite teachers, Big Brother/Big Sister volunteers, responsible peers, little league trainers, or next door neighbors (see Figure 5.2).

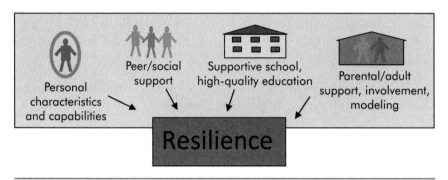

Figure 5.2 Different elements contribute to the development of effective adaptation systems. Stronger adaptation systems support the individual's resiliency

Effective and involved parenting is important to alleviate the effects of the environment and life circumstances on the development of resilience in children who demonstrate many of the risk factors for adverse developmental outcomes. Parental dysfunction due to substance abuse, lack of resources (severe poverty, for example), immature teenage parenting, or unavailability (such as during a divorce process or long working hours) can cause a child to feel lonely, less supported, and more vulnerable emotionally, physically, and socially (Masten and Reed 2002; Masten *et al.* 1990; Werner 2000). Close bonding with primary caregivers and having a supportive family and school network increase the likelihood of a better developmental outcome, and act as major protective factors.

These research findings are not unexpected. Optimally, parents shape these skills and support their children on emotional and practical levels. They provide guidance, nurture coping skills, and prepare their children to deal with adversity. Through socializing experiences, children learn important skills such as waiting, sharing, judging, negotiating, asking for help, solving problems, avoiding conflicts, and self-regulation (controlling their emotions, thoughts, and behaviors). Secure attachment between parents and children sets the foundation for a sense of trust, responsibility, empathy for others, and self-worth. The family becomes the model for relationships that guides the child's expectation in future relationships. Studies indicate that children who have parents available for an attached relationship become more resilient than those who do not have available caregivers (Werner 2000). When individuals in the immediate family are not available or capable of providing appropriate socializing and support, other adults, such as relatives, teachers, or volunteers, can fill the role to nurture and support the development of the adaptation systems of the child.

Pleasure in mastery adaptation system

The acquisition of a new skill brings pleasure and satisfaction that motivates people to learn other new skills. A person who has mastered a new dance movement takes pleasure in that success and is motivated to participate in the following class, or engage in the next challenging step. A well-developed pleasure in mastery adaptation system encourages people to take on further learning risks (Lewis 1999; Masten and Coatsworth 1998). This motivation becomes very beneficial to the individual when facing challenges, since coping and adjusting require learning. For example, the first day at a new school, riding a new bicycle, or moving to a new home all require the acquisition of new skills. An adult who is confident and motivated to learn and manage a new computer program introduced at work may hold the job more securely than a co-worker who is anxious and avoids learning the new program.

School and after-school activities provide constant opportunities to increase a person's sense of mastery and motivation. Success in academic and non-academic assignments at school or in after-school programs (such as dancing, sports, drama) reveals hidden competencies that can be appreciated by others and provide children, especially those who are academically challenged, with opportunities to support the mastery motivational system (Brooks 1999).

Some individuals with autism have limited academic competencies and are less successful in leisure activities, such as sports or the arts. They are less likely to experience success and mastery and, as a consequence, do not develop the pleasure in mastery adaptation system. When facing new tasks, they may exhibit avoidance or disruptive behaviors due to anxiety and uncomfortable feelings associated with learning.

RESILIENCE-PROMOTING INTERVENTION FOR INDIVIDUALS WITH AUTISM

There are many strategies and principles derived from research studies that are currently used to foster resilience in children at risk (Batmanghelidjh 1999; Nettles, Mucherah and Jones 2000). Following are descriptions of these strategies and principles, adapted to the needs of individuals with autism and developmental disabilities. The strategies are divided into seven categories, and many of them are related to specific activities in the activities chapters of this book. The seven categories are as follows:

- self-regulation
- pleasure in mastery adaptation system
- pre-test before new activities
- change attributions about mistakes and failures
- increase autonomy
- teach general information
- increase personal connectedness at home, in school, and in the community.

We shall now look at each of these categories in turn.

Self-regulation

Effective self-regulation enables individuals to *keep cool* when stressful situations occur. Teaching relaxation strategies to individuals with autism enables them to achieve control over their own behaviors. Relaxation and imagery procedures were found to decrease disruptive, stereotypic, and self-injurious behaviors in individuals with autism (Groden and LeVasseur 1995; Groden *et al.* 1988). At the Groden Center, students with a wide range of capabilities are taught to use relaxation and imagery techniques as stress reduction strategies (Cautela and Groden 1978; Groden and Cautela 1984; Groden and LeVasseur 1995).

Pleasure in mastery adaptation system

Finding out what we are good at and receiving support from the people around us helps everyone on the road to success. Realizing that our efforts result in success can motivate new learning as outlined in these techniques:

- *Identify and nurture special abilities and talents:* islands of competence are special abilities and talents (Brooks 1999). These islands can be present even when the individual faces difficulties in other areas of functioning. For example, some individuals with autism have a special talent in the arts, while others are very good at taking care of animals. These competencies can be nurtured to provide the individual with a source of joy, satisfaction, and self-actualization (Brooks 1999; Brooks and Goldstein 2001). In addition, these activities may lead to expressions of appreciation from others, nurturing further opportunities to develop resilience, self-efficacy, and self-esteem. Some of the special capabilities that can be nurtured and appreciated by others are listed in Table 5.2.

Table 5.2 Examples of areas of special capabilities and talents that can be explored

Areas	Activities
Visual arts	Drawing, painting, sculpturing, photography, beading
Music	Playing instruments, collecting compact discs, collecting newspaper articles about singers
Organization	Arranging books in the library, helping a teacher arrange materials for teaching, filling out the attendance list, acting as the reminder for following schedules
Horticulture	Gardening, flower arranging, potting plants, decorating pots
Taking care of others	Taking care of animals, reading or playing with children, babysitting
Cooking	With supervision if needed
Technical capabilities	Fixing broken furniture, operating a video camera
Special academic interests	Medicine, astronomy, computers, animal care
Helping others	Participating in activities such as the Meals on Wheels program, helping at home, volunteering in the church, preschool, or nursing home, and helping with fundraising

- *Set high but reasonable expectations:* realistic expectations support the pleasure in mastery adaptation system (Lewis 1999). Goals that are unrealistically high lead to failure, while goals that are too easily reached do not challenge the student enough to promote a sense of real accomplishment. Using pre-tests to assess a student on a curriculum and placing the student at the correct step will help to provide the proper challenge. Providing a realistic challenge will lead to success.

- *Encourage the individual to learn new skills:* when teaching a new skill, increase students' awareness of the novelty inherent in this skill by labeling it as a *new skill*. New skills can be as simple as opening a jar, adding a new picture on the communication board, using a different kind of brush in art class, or taking a different route to the gym. By increasing the students' awareness of their ability to learn new skills, their sense of mastery and motivation to learn will also increase.

- *Divide activities into small steps:* each complex task that is taught to individuals with autism and developmental disabilities can be simplified by dividing it into small steps. Breaking activities into discrete actions is referred to as task analysis. Task analysis allows the individual to notice success in each step of a task, even if the whole assignment cannot be accomplished, especially in the early stages of the learning process.

- *Emphasize linkage between the individual's efforts and success:* parents and teachers can provide verbal and visual input to help children realize the connection between their efforts and their outcomes. For example, videotaping children performing an activity, or taking photos of the process and presenting it, can help them make sense of the whole process that they have accomplished. Using a progressive chart or table can also be a helpful guide in monitoring successful progress. Positive verbal and visual feedback about a person's success builds the pleasure in mastery adaptation system.

- *Find opportunities to celebrate success:* many typically developing individuals enjoy receiving trophies, medals, certificates, and bumper stickers, honoring their participation in activities and their successes. These symbols help them continue their efforts and lead to accomplishments, which impact on their self-worth. Activities for individuals with developmental disabilities should be designed to emphasize and highlight their success. Displaying visible objects at home such as trophies or certificates can result in feelings of self-worth and pride.

Pre-test before new activities

When presenting new activities to a person who has autism or developmental disabilities, parents and teachers should first assess the individual's skill on the task. Start where the person is, and move forward so that time is not spent on teaching something the person already knows. Have students do as much as possible on their own to give them a feeling of responsibility.

Change attributions about mistakes and failures

Mistakes and failures are part of learning and growing and should be attributed as such in order to encourage a positive approach to learning. Parents and teachers can model this approach by talking about their own mistakes and disappointments, and responding in a positive and encouraging manner when correcting their students' mistakes. Mistakes and failures can be a growing experience for a student if used sensitively by the parent or the teacher to do the following:

- Analyze what can be done better next time. For example, if a student did not study for a quiz, next time she can study and might score better.

- Do a *reality check* (review expectations with the student and determine if they are realistic). For example, if the student is upset for not being chosen for the leading role in a play, he should not assume that the teacher doesn't like him. It should be pointed out that many students were interested in this role and that only one could be picked.

- Figure out the person's interests and motivation by analyzing his or her cause for disappointment. For example, if a student is disappointed for not being selected for the school's baseball team, the main motivation can be social, or interest in baseball, or both. Each reason can be handled differently.

- Change attributions about failure. Teach the notion that everybody makes mistakes.

- Reinforce efforts, cooperation, asking for help, and helping others, rather than the results.

- Practice acceptance of positive criticism.

- Practice positive and supportive judgment of self and others.

- Empower the individual to communicate on topics that can lead to unnecessary pain and disappointment, as shown in the following example:

   Brianna, a student who has motor and sensory challenges, refused to participate in physical education classes. A discussion with her mother revealed that the gym teacher often assigned captains to recruit their teams. Because she was always the last one to be picked, Brianna's physical education classes became a source of social humiliation. Brianna's mother encouraged her to share her perception with the physical education teacher. The impact of this conversation with her teacher changed the way students were assigned to teams, strengthened Brianna's belief in her ability to tackle difficulties, and reduced her use of avoidance strategies.

Some students are limited in their abilities to comprehend and express their thoughts. Using picture rehearsal strategies can help them practice scenes that deal with mistakes and disappointments.

Increase autonomy

It is important to support a sense of autonomy and self-determination in individuals with autism and developmental disabilities by encouraging them to make and execute their own choices (Clark *et al.* 2004). To do this, it is necessary not only to provide them with the knowledge about available options, but also to teach effective expressions of their preferences and choices. Opportunities for choice should match the developmental level of the individual. The following are suggestions for choice making:

- foods, drinks and snacks

- activities for leisure

- schedule options

- books for reading assignments
- materials to use for handwriting practice
- living arrangements
- budgeting money
- vocational opportunities.

Teach general information

Many students with autism and developmental disabilities are very anxious about events that are often unavoidable such as going to the dentist, the physician, or the hairdresser. Using picture rehearsal and relaxation, and providing general knowledge to help them understand, rationalize, and know what to expect and how to react, may reduce their concerns and help them view the experience differently, as illustrated in the following examples:

> Scott, a four-year-old toddler, became anxious every time he saw a garbage truck. In such instances, he would become withdrawn, tense, walk away, and engage in self-talking and self-stimulation. Often he would turn around and look at the truck and appear worried. His mother decided to try reducing his worries by teaching him about the truck. She borrowed books from the library about garbage trucks and used simple words to explain the functions of the truck. Together, they put garbage into the container and watched the driver take it. They waved goodbye to the truck every time it left their premises. Scott learned to feel better about garbage trucks because he became exposed to them frequently and realized that they do not harm him, and he also gained knowledge about the purpose of the garbage truck.

> Justin, a student with Asperger syndrome, was very negative about participating in group relaxation, referring to it as *stupid*. Teaching him about the effects of stress and relaxation on his breathing, heart rate, and asthma increased his cooperation.

The opportunity to learn more and increase skills in areas that are problematic can reduce stress and lead to better coping strategies which increase resilience.

Increase personal connectedness at home, in school, and in the community

Studies on inclusive educational systems found that a supportive and positive atmosphere between typically developing students and students with learning disabilities and other special needs can be promoted by encouraging and reinforcing positive behaviors such as:

- recognizing and valuing students who help or befriend others
- emphasizing a less competitive atmosphere
- having teachers model acceptance of differences
- valuing acts of kindness and support toward students who have special needs (Fiedler and Simpson 1987; Fisher, Pumpian and Sax 1998).

The struggles and the needs of families raising children with autism and developmental disabilities are beyond what many can imagine. Families are extremely vulnerable emotionally, physically, financially, and socially, and can benefit tremendously from support (Dumas *et al.* 1991; Higgins, Bailey and Pearce 2005). Stress in families is often high due to challenges related to the child's behaviors and needs, increased workload and demands in and out of the home, concerns relating to the future of the child, loss of income due to inability to work outside of the home, lack of sleep associated with the child's different circadian rhythm, social and leisure limitations, and difficulties in being accepted by family members and others in the community. Facing judgmental attitudes from others, including professionals, leaves caregivers with more trauma than support (Klauber 1998).

For many parents, school is the primary community organization with which they can partner in the care and support of their child. For school professionals, working with parents who often carry an extreme burden may also be difficult. A school culture that values and actively nurtures interaction between students with developmental disabilities, their families, and the staff can provide a powerful support system to both sides. As such, it can help parents and teachers function as a team to help their children. Educating school personnel on the unique needs and difficulties related to raising a child with autism and developmental disabilities, and having parents share their perspectives with the staff can establish an open, non-judgmental, and supportive attitude.

Activities that can support a sense of community between parents and school include the following:

- parents volunteering to help teachers in classrooms, or to help organize activities and events
- developing a phone directory for parents to create a social network
- scheduling lectures and workshops that can provide parents with strategies on how to help their child with behavior problems, emotional developmental issues, and coping with school demands
- creating a list of recommended resources and service providers (dentists, pediatricians, optometrists, etc.)
- providing or referring parents to social support groups
- providing or sharing information with parents on educational workshops and conferences
- providing home-based services to educate parents and assist with behavioral problems
- holding social events at school, such as open houses, talent shows, and seasonal celebrations, to provide a sense of community
- providing respite to allow parents the opportunity to have free time
- providing food baskets or toys for the children at holidays.

THE EXPECTED RESILIENCE OUTCOME IN INDIVIDUALS WITH AUTISM

A person's resilience is expressed by reaching a satisfactory developmental outcome despite his or her background struggle. What is a satisfactory developmental outcome for individuals with autism? Research often focuses on outcomes, such as meeting cultural and age expectations, reduced psychopathological issues, or increased academic achievements. For those diagnosed with high-functioning autism, resilience will be demonstrated by reaching high academic achievements, maintaining successful employment, and tolerating work-related social demands. For individuals who are more profoundly impacted by autism, different criteria and qualifiers of resiliency must be used. For these individuals, demonstrating resilience could be the ability to express and execute positive preferences and choices, showing willingness to learn and experience novelties, maintaining a strong support system, and demonstrating self-regulation and self-control under stress.

CONCLUSION

Resilience is a key component in reaching effective adaptation and successful coping with life challenges. Individuals with autism are faced with unique social, cognitive, physiological, and behavioral challenges that pose obstacles to the development of their adaptation system, and make them more vulnerable to the effects of adversities. However, resilience can be fostered in students with autism at all levels of functioning by nurturing self-regulation, increasing opportunities to experience success, autonomy, and independence, and by increasing problem-solving skills and general knowledge.

Table 6.1 Activities that promote optimism

Name of activity	Description of activity	Approx. time of activity	Also related to: Humor (H) Self-Efficacy (SE) Kindness (K) Resilience (R)	Potential content area application*
Positive affirmations	Reading positive statements written by others	5 minutes	H, SE, K, R	C, L, S
Positive scanning	Making positive observations about upcoming events	10–30 minutes	SE, R	C, L
Positive expectations	Expressing expectations about events that might happen during the day	10–20 minutes	SE, R	C, L
Racing toward optimism	Interactive game that encourages expressing optimistic views about daily school activities	5–10 minutes each day over a week	SE	C, L, M
Incorporating principles of optimism into a picture rehearsal script	Using picture rehearsal scenes to cope with stressful events	5 minutes	R	C, L, S
What optimism is and what it isn't	Differentiating between optimistic and pessimistic interpretations of situations	30–60 minutes	R	C, L, S
Dealing with my problems in the most optimistic way	Learning to assess the nature and magnitude of a problem	20–30 minutes	R	C, L, S

*Communication (C); language arts (L); math and science (M); social skills (S); physical education and motor skills (P); vocational and community skills (V)

Chapter 6

Activities that Promote Optimism

Table 6.1 on the opposite page lists the optimism activities described in this chapter in relation to the other four areas of positive psychology: humor, self-efficacy, kindness, and resilience.

POSITIVE AFFIRMATIONS

Instructional format

Individual student or small group.

Learning objective

Participants will increase their positive outlooks and expectations by acknowledging a positive personal trait and linking it to events that have taken place or will take place in the future.

Potential content area application

Communication; language arts; social skills.

Materials

Index cards; bulletin board with the names/pictures of each student (leaving room to tack positive affirmation cards underneath).

Procedure

1. Identify positive traits that the students have and write individualized positive affirmations onto index cards. These affirmations will be recited by the students to promote the development of self-awareness of their positive attributes. Examples of positive affirmations:

   o 'I am a good friend. At lunch I share my cookies with others.'

   o 'I take good care of my things. At school I hang my coat neatly in my locker.'

   o 'I am helpful to others. When it is time for a snack, I can get the plates and cups.'

2. Read each student's positive affirmations aloud and post them onto the bulletin board under their name/picture. Tell the students the board will remain up and they will be giving themselves a star whenever they demonstrate the positive affirmation. The bulletin board will serve as a visual cue to the students about the frequency with which they display their positive attributes.

3. Rehearse with the students specific scripted affirmations prior to events that will present an opportunity to demonstrate the targeted positive attribute.

POSITIVE SCANNING

Instructional format

Individual student or small group.

Learning objective

Participants will increase their positive outlook about events and different environments by looking for positive components.

Potential content area application

Communication; language arts.

Materials

Things I Look Forward To Worksheet (page 94).

Procedure

1. Just prior to an activity, describe the activity to the students.

2. Hand out the Things I Look Forward To Worksheet (page 94) and ask the students to fill out what they anticipate they will like about the activity.

3. Have the students read what they are looking forward to and create a list of the positive features such as, 'I am looking forward to getting on the bus because it is fun to look out of the window' or, 'Mike likes birthdays because of the candy.'

4. After the activity, ask the students to make a list of what they did, what they enjoyed, and why they look forward to another activity. For example, 'I liked going on the bus to a new place' or, 'I look forward to field trips because I know I will have fun.'

Modification

- Create a booklet of positive observations to send home to parents and encourage the parents to remind their child about them.

- Keep an ongoing graph in the classroom and allow students to write and post their positive reflections on their experiences.

Evaluation

Record notes regarding the expectations expressed by the student.

Things I Look Forward To Worksheet

WHY I LOOK FORWARD TO . . .

 . . . Riding the bus*

....
....
....

   *OR:

- Being with my friends

- Being at home

- Going out for recess

- Having a birthday party

- Going grocery shopping

- Playing with a pet

POSITIVE EXPECTATIONS

Instructional format

Individual student or small group.

Learning objective

Participants will increase their positive outlook and expectations by making optimistic observations of preferred events during the day.

Potential content area application

Communication; language arts.

Materials

Daily written or picture schedule; happy face or star stickers.

Procedure

1. In the morning, after presenting the day's schedule to the students, ask them what activity they are most excited about or expect to be the most fun.

2. Have each student place a sticker next to that activity on the schedule. As they attach the sticker, ask them to state why they are most excited about that activity.

3. At the end of the day, refer back to the schedule, have the students locate the activities they highlighted, and ask them to make a positive statement about the activity. For example, 'I got to make delicious brownies in cooking group.'

Modification

- Have the students keep a diary of future events recording their positive expectations about the events.

- Send home a booklet of the child's positive expectations so that the parents can read it to their child.

Evaluation

Collect the positive expectations expressed by the students and record notes about them.

RACING TOWARD OPTIMISM

Instructional format

Individual student or small group.

Learning objective

Participants will increase their positive outlook and expectations by making optimistic observations of preferred events during the day.

Potential content area application

Communication; language arts; math and science (counting spots on the board).

Materials

Fun Activity Cards, cut out and laminated (page 98); Racing Toward Optimism race track board with race car, cut out and laminated (page 99).

Procedure

1. Ask the students to choose a Fun Activity Card that represents a fun daily activity that they will be participating in that day.
2. Have the students attach their cards to the race track board in the Start position.
3. Guide the students in selecting an award they will receive when the race car reaches the Finish.

4. Go around the class and ask each student to name what they expect to be fun about their chosen activity. For each optimistic statement, move the race car forward one space on the track. Continue until the race car reaches the Finish.

5. At the end of the day, review the fun activities that happened.

Modification

Use stickers in place of Fun Activity Cards.

Evaluation

Evaluate students on their ability to predict fun things that could happen to them during the day.

Fun Activity Cards

Playground

Field trip

Gym

Making puzzles

Computer

Artwork

Playing with toys

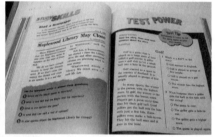

Reading

Snack

Racing Toward Optimism

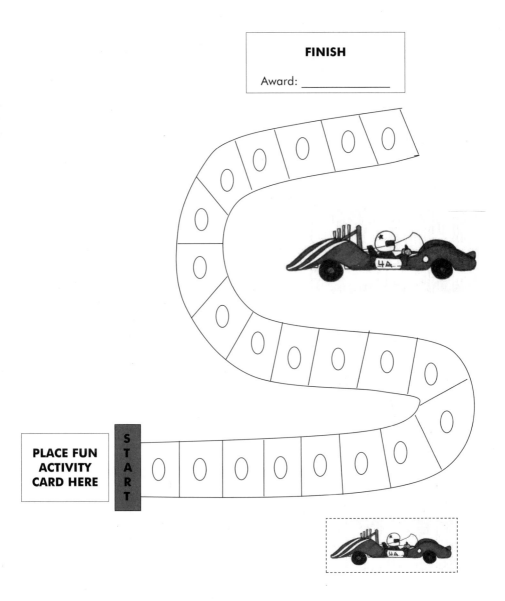

FINISH

Award: _____

PLACE FUN
ACTIVITY
CARD HERE

START

✓

INCORPORATING PRINCIPLES OF OPTIMISM INTO A PICTURE REHEARSAL SCRIPT

Instructional format

Individual student.

Learning objective

Participants will increase their positive outlook and expectations by identifying positive beliefs and attributions when something stressful occurs.

Potential content area application

Communication; language arts; social skills.

Materials

Cards with cognitive picture rehearsal scripts (see Figure 6.1 for an example).

Procedure

1. Create a picture rehearsal script which incorporates a positive outlook, for example:

   ○ First card: 'I am going on a field trip to pick out a pumpkin.'

   ○ Second card: 'It's hard to wait, but I can do it.'

   ○ Third card: 'I take a deep breath and relax.'

   ○ Fourth card: 'We are on the bus to the pumpkin field.'

   ○ Fifth card: 'I know I will find a beautiful pumpkin.'

   ○ Sixth card: 'I found just the right pumpkin and I like it.'

   ○ Seventh card: 'This was a fun-filled trip.'

   ○ Eighth card: 'Now I imagine _____'

2. Sit next to or across from the student and establish attention. Assess that the student is calm and ready for instruction.

3. Present each picture card and read the script to the student, pointing to the important features in the pictures. Practicing key phrases of the script such as, 'It's hard to wait, but I can do it,' during relevant activities will assist the student in using the skill functionally. Progress until the script is finished.

4. Hand the picture cards to the student and ask the student to read or repeat the script.

5. Practice the picture rehearsal scripts daily, changing the specifics as needed (i.e., describing the next field trip) at scheduled times. When introducing a new script, it should be practiced at least two or three times each day.

6. When the student becomes familiar with the script, it can be introduced prior to a relevant event.

Note: Children with cognitive or language deficits can use sign language, gestures, facial expressions or verbal approximations to express the scene or demonstrate their understanding of the pictures.

Modification

- Ask the student to suggest a future event that will be challenging and involve the student in developing a picture rehearsal script.

- Ask the student to verbalize how to handle future mistakes, what to say, what to do, and so on.

Evaluation

- Keep anecdotal notes about the student's attention and participation.

- Evaluate the student's ability to use the strategies from the script in real situations.

Cognitive picture rehearsal script: waiting for a reinforcer	I'm in my classroom 
It is almost time for me to earn my reinforcer for having a great day! 	I have to wait for my teacher to come back to the classroom. I am a patient person. *Challenging event = waiting; also a positive affirmation* 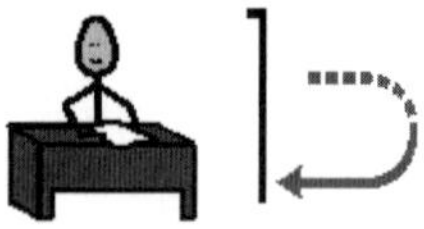
I take a deep breath and relax. I say to myself, 'I can wait a minute or two.' *Stress reducer = deep breath* 	I know that my teacher is very busy and has lots to do. My teacher will return soon to give me my reinforcer. *Impersonal and temporary* 
I decide to look at a book while I wait. *Coping strategy* 	My teacher comes back. I did a good job waiting, so now I enjoy . . . (insert something reinforcing for the student). *Positive reinforcement* 

Figure 6.1 Cognitive picture rehearsal script: waiting for a reinforcer

Source: The Picture Communication Symbols © 1981–2010 by DynaVox Mayer-Johnson LLC. All Rights Reserved Worldwide. Used with permission.

WHAT OPTIMISM IS AND WHAT IT ISN'T

Instructional format

Individual student or small group.

Learning objective

This activity is based on *The Optimistic Child* written by Dr. Seligman and colleagues. The activity provides scenarios with two different interpretations (optimistic and pessimistic). The participants will learn how the interpretation of a situation can affect their feelings and that choosing the optimistic interpretation will make them feel good.

Potential content area application

Communication; language arts; social skills.

Materials

Problem Board (see Figure 6.2 for an example) and Situation Scenes (pages 105–107).

Procedure

1. Draw your own Problem Board, based on the example shown in Figure 6.2, and display it so that the students can easily see it.

2. From the Situation Scenes provided, cut out the picture with the text, and the optimistic and pessimistic responses.

3. Attach the picture to The Problem space on the Problem Board and read the problem to the students.

4. Read the optimistic and pessimistic responses to the students. Help the students figure out which thoughts are optimistic ones and which are pessimistic ones.

5. Ask the students to place the responses in the appropriate spot on the Problem Board.

Modification

Ask the student to fill out the Situations I Have to Deal With Sometimes Worksheet (page 108) and create individualized scenes from that information.

Evaluation

Take anecdotal notes to monitor the student's attributions.

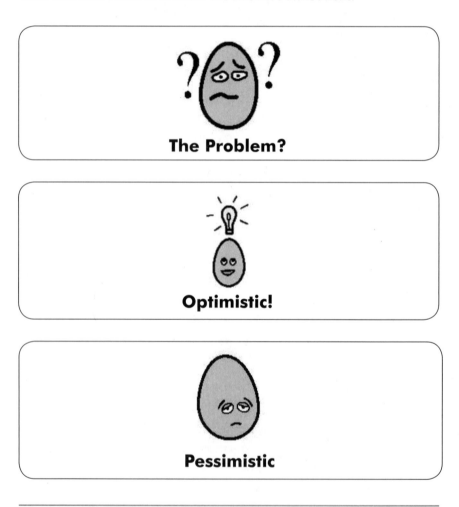

Figure 6.2 Problem board

Source: The Picture Communication Symbols © 1981–2010 by DynaVox Mayer-Johnson LLC. All Rights Reserved Worldwide. Used with permission.

Situation Scene 1

Dylan sees his friends cooking together, he crosses the room and they do not seem to notice him.

'My friends don't like me!'	'My friends are busy. I can wait, listen, and then slowly join in!'

Situation Scene 2

Chester's big brother reprimands him for breaking the window.

'My brother always picks on me!'	'My brother is just upset right now because I broke the window.'

✓

Situation Scene 3

Mother asks Benjamin to clean the garage.

'Cleaning the garage is too hard! I can never finish it!'	'Mom needs help. It's my responsibility to help and I can do it!'

Situation Scene 4

Sara is invited to a party. There will be many people she won't know at the party.

'I am not going to this party! This will be a boring party!'	'I can enjoy the food and the music. Maybe I can meet new friends who are fun!'

✓

Situation Scene 5

David made mistakes on his test.

'I never do well on tests!'	'I did not do well on this test. Everybody makes mistakes. I can handle it!'

Situation Scene 6

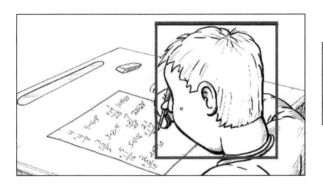

The teacher gave Matthew hard math homework.

'It is too hard. I can't do it.'	'The homework is hard, but I can be patient. I can have my (mother, father, sister) help me and I will finish it.'

✓

Situations I Have to Deal with Sometimes Worksheet

(Draw picture of situation here)

This is NOT an optimistic or positive way to think about my situation: _____

_____

This makes me feel: _____

_____

This IS an optimistic or positive way to think about my situation: _____

_____

This makes me feel: _____

_____

✓

DEALING WITH MY PROBLEMS IN THE MOST OPTIMISTIC WAY

Instructional format

Individual student or small group.

Learning objective

Participants will develop problem-solving skills by breaking problems down into small manageable steps, and creating solutions based on optimism.

Potential content area application

Communication; language arts; social skills.

Materials

Dealing with My Problems Worksheet (page 111).

Procedure

1. Present the students with an issue that is frequently problematic to them, or that results in their behavior upsetting others.

2. Use the Dealing with My Problems Worksheet to guide the students through the evaluation of the problem and develop ideas to solve the problem.

3. Help the students state the problem in their own words. For some students it will be better to narrow the problem down as much as possible. For example, 'Everyone cuts in front of me and I never get to go first!' poses two problems: (1) people cutting in front of the student, and (2) the student never gets to go first. Each of the problems can be dealt with separately.

4. The questions on the worksheet focus on the aspects of permanence of the problem (is it permanent or temporary?), pervasiveness (is it global or specific?), or personalized (is it personal or impersonal?).

5. Help the students find solutions based on the optimistic assessment. Not all the strategies need to be good or realistic ideas. Expression of unrealistic ideas can be an opportunity to teach the student logical thinking and judgment.

Modification

Modify the questions specific to the problem.

Evaluation

Evaluate the students' responses and the students' use of problem solving in real-life situations.

Dealing with My Problems Worksheet

What is the problem?
> Example: 'I left the sneakers at home that I need for gym.'

Assessing the problem. Is the problem . . .
> **. . . permanent or temporary?**
> Example: Temporary. 'I usually bring my sneakers to school. I can forget once in a while.'

> **. . . global or specific?**
> Example: Specific. 'It's just my gym shoes.'

> **. . . personal or impersonal?**
> Example: Impersonal. 'Other children sometimes forget their sneakers. I can borrow a pair for today from the gym teacher.'

Is it your fault?

How can you avoid the problem?

Is it good to avoid the problem?

How big is the problem?
1 = Very big; 2 = Big; 3 = Not so big; 4 = A small problem, really! 5 = Not a problem at all

Think about ideas to solve the problem.

✓

Table 7.1 Activities that promote humor

Name of activity	Description of activity	Approx. time of activity	Also related to: Optimism (O) Self-Efficacy (SE) Kindness (K) Resilience (R)	Potential content area application*
Flying balloons	A playful activity using balloons	10–15 minutes		C, P
Funny faces	Creating funny faces using photographs and crayons	30–60 minutes		C, L, P
Monkeys jumping on the bed	Re-enactment of a funny story	30–45 minutes	K	C, L, M, P
Cloudy with a chance of meatballs	Learning to recognize and enjoy humor in stories	30–45 minutes		C, L, M
Funny pictures	Identifying what is funny in a picture	15–30 minutes		C, L, M, S, P
Animal surprise!	Imitating animal movements and sounds. Creating mis-matched animal combinations	10–20 minutes		C, L
Simon says	Imitating funny body movements and sounds as determined by a leader	20 minutes or more	K	C, L, S, P
Comic strips	Learning how to interpret comic strips	30–45 minutes		C, L, M
Joke of the day	Practicing telling jokes	5 minutes		C, L, M

*Communication (C); language arts (L); math and science (M); social skills (S); physical education and motor skills (P); vocational and community skills (V)

Chapter 7

Activities that Promote Humor

Table 7.1 on the opposite page lists the humor activities described in this chapter in relation to the other four areas of positive psychology: optimism, self-efficacy, kindness, and resilience.

FLYING BALLOONS

Instructional format

Small group.

Learning objective

Participants will learn to enjoy humor by engaging in a silly, playful activity. This activity is aimed at modeling laughter and other humoristic responses by watching balloons fly. The participants are encouraged to be playful.

Potential content area application

Communication; physical education and motor skills.

Precautions

Latex allergy; choking hazard.

Materials

Balloons and string; helium (optional); Evaluation Form for Humor Activities (page 115); Scoring Rubric (page 116).

Procedure

1. Inflate several balloons, knot them and tie strings to them. Show the students how balloons fly in the air by bouncing the balloons or pulling the balloons around by their string.

2. Model expressions of humor such as smiling, laughing, and excitement as the balloons are bouncing in the air.

3. Ask each student to imitate the balloons.

4. For some of the balloons, inflate them but don't knot them. Let the balloons deflate while pinching the opening so that it makes a squeaking sound. Point out the sound to the students.

5. Model expressions of humor as the balloons make the squeaking sound.

6. Ask each student to imitate a balloon deflating and making a squeaking sound.

7. Model laughter and expressions of joy.

8. Closure activity: ask the children to share what they enjoyed most about the activity.

Evaluation

Evaluate the students using the Evaluation Form for Humor Activities (page 115) and Scoring Rubric (page 116). Other appropriate skills, such as imitation, can be added to the final two columns in the table.

Evaluation Form for Humor Activities

Date:

Activity:

Duration of the activity:

Student name	Participation level	Attention level	Response level	Expression of humor	Skill: _____	Skill: _____
	1 2 3	1 2 3	1 2 3	1 2 3	1 2 3	1 2 3
	1 2 3	1 2 3	1 2 3	1 2 3	1 2 3	1 2 3
	1 2 3	1 2 3	1 2 3	1 2 3	1 2 3	1 2 3
	1 2 3	1 2 3	1 2 3	1 2 3	1 2 3	1 2 3
	1 2 3	1 2 3	1 2 3	1 2 3	1 2 3	1 2 3
	1 2 3	1 2 3	1 2 3	1 2 3	1 2 3	1 2 3
	1 2 3	1 2 3	1 2 3	1 2 3	1 2 3	1 2 3

Comments:

Scoring Rubric

	1	2	3
Participation	Does not take part in the activity, ignores it, tries to move away or anxiously distances him/herself from the activity, does not keep eye contact to observe, does not seem to listen (no need to document other rubrics)	Observes and takes some part in the activity	Participates in most of the activity
Attention level	Attends to the activity for 40% of the time or less	Attends to the activity for about 50–75% of the time	Attends to the activity for 75% of the time or more, or completes the assignment satisfactorily
Response level	Does not take part in the activity	Shows capacity for engaging in the activity with support and one-on-one modeling	Shows facial expressions paired with motor behaviors appropriate to the activity (clapping, swaying to music, turning pages, etc.)
Expression of humor	Student does not respond with humor to the activity	Student expresses enjoyment from participation in the activity	Student expresses enjoyment from the incongruity presented

Skill:

Skill:

FUNNY FACES

Instructional format

Individual or small group.

Learning objective

Participants will learn to enjoy humor and incongruency by looking at and creating silly funny faces using a flip book. The book combines eyes, noses and mouths which get mixed up to produce funny faces. In addition to learning about humor, students learn to label facial features and become flexible by looking at facial variations.

Potential content area application

Communication (sequencing); language arts; art; physical education and motor skills (body parts).

Materials

Digital camera; printer; laminator; scissors; ring binder; hole punch.

Procedure

1. Ask students to make funny faces, such as sticking out their tongues, closing their eyes, opening their eyes widely, etc.

2. Take a portrait picture of each student's face.

3. Download pictures and enlarge or reduce the pictures as needed so that they are all approximately the same size. Print out the pictures and laminate.

4. Using scissors (or paper cutter) cut each portrait into three sections: (1) eyes and above, (2) nose, (3) mouth and below.

5. Hole punch each of the sections and arrange them in a ring binder to create a book of faces.

6. Present the book to the students and have them turn the pages to create funny combinations. Support their exploration of what is funny about the faces they make.

Modification

1. Review the Funny Faces Template (page 119) with the students, pointing to the areas designated to each facial feature.

2. Using facial features cut from the students' portrait photographs, or stickers or drawings, demonstrate how to place the eyes, nose, and mouth in the correct areas.

3. Provide cut facial features to the students and have them glue them to a piece of paper. Encourage them to add other body parts by drawing arms, legs, etc. (see Figure 7.1 for examples).

4. Ask the students to show the result of their work. Be explicit by describing what is funny about the faces.

Evaluation

Evaluate the students using the Evaluation Form for Humor Activities (page 115) and Scoring Rubric (page 116). The teacher can also document ability to use fine motor skills by the student identifying facial features (e.g. by pointing) and/or constructing a face.

Funny Faces Template

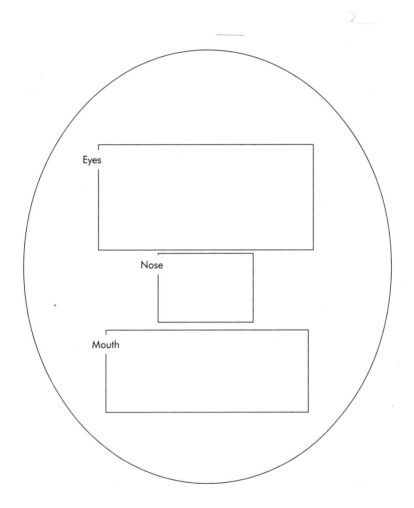

Eyes

Nose

Mouth

Figure 7.1 Examples of facial collages that were displayed in the classroom to give enjoyment to the students. Crayons were used to add details

MONKEYS JUMPING ON THE BED

Instructional format

Small group.

Learning objective

Participants will learn to enjoy humor in stories and engage in silly, playful activities.

Potential content area application

Communication (sequencing); language arts; math and science (numbers and numbers sense); physical education and motor skills (gross motor).

Precaution

This activity should be conducted on floor mats to avoid injury.

Materials

Mattress; floor mats (placed around the mattress); pillows; a blanket or sheet; Eileen Christelow's book *Five Little Monkeys Jumping on the Bed*.

Procedure

1. Begin the activity by reading *Five Little Monkeys Jumping on the Bed*. Once the story has been read, ask the students if they would like to be monkeys.

2. Make a bed using the mattress, pillows and a blanket or sheet.

3. Ask the students to sit or kneel on the bed.

4. Reread the story and have the students act out the story as it is being read, asking them to imitate the monkeys (for safety, instead of jumping on the bed, ask the students to wave their arms in the air). The teacher should call out each student's name in turn, and ask them to fall or roll off the bed. As each student rolls off the bed, have the student join in the refrain of 'No more monkeys

jumping on the bed.' Laughter should occur when pretending to be monkeys, and falling off the bed and singing the refrain.

5. Closure: the children can pretend to go to sleep.

Note: If individual students have difficulty sustaining participation in this activity, try pairing them with a peer, or let them be the first or the last monkey to fall, or let them sit and watch.

Modification

- Attach the story characters to a felt board with Velcro. Assign a student to each monkey on the felt board. While reading the story, each time a monkey falls off the bed, have the student take his or her monkey off the board and then count how many monkeys have fallen down.

- Have students listen to the story and song on tape.

- Make monkey masks, tails, or puppets.

Evaluation

Evaluate the students using the Evaluation Form for Humor Activities (page 115) and Scoring Rubric (page 116).

CLOUDY WITH A CHANCE OF MEATBALLS

Instructional format

Small group.

Learning objective

Participants will learn to enjoy humor and incongruency in stories.

This activity is provided as an example of how to use funny books to teach humor and flexible thinking.

Potential content area application

Communication; language arts; math and science (size, quantity, weather).

Materials

Judi Barrett's book *Cloudy with a Chance of Meatballs*; weather calendar; weather symbols (sun, clouds, rain, snow); a pre-made hat with dogs and cats pasted to it; plain hats; glue; assorted pictures to attach to plain hats; crayons; markers.

Procedure

1. Help the students determine the current weather. Ask one student to put the appropriate weather symbol on the weather calendar.

2. Read the book *Cloudy with a Chance of Meatballs* introducing metaphors while reading (e.g., it's raining cats and dogs), and emphasize the incongruency.

3. After reading the book, ask the students to suggest other things that would be silly if they rained from the sky.

4. Pull out a silly hat with cats and dogs attached to it and ask the students if they want to make a silly hat.

5. Give each student a plain hat, assorted pictures, and glue. Have them pick out the pictures they would like to attach to the hat.

6. When they are finished making their hats, bring the students together in a circle and ask them to share their hats and describe what rained onto the hat.

Modification

Instead of hats, use umbrellas and string, and dangle items from the umbrella.

Evaluation

Evaluate the students using the Evaluation Form for Humor Activities (page 115) and Scoring Rubric (page 116).

FUNNY PICTURES

Instructional format

Individual student or small group.

Learning objective

Participants will learn to enjoy humor by recognizing incongruency presented in pictures.

Potential content area application

Communication; language arts; math and science (sequencing); social skills; physical education and motor skills. Understanding incongruency and responding to it overtly and in a socially appropriate manner requires two different skills, cognitive and social. This activity nurtures both skills by using pictures that depict incongruence and absurdity related to people or things.

Materials

Photographs, cartoons or funny images reflecting incongruence or the unexpected that can be found in kids books, magazines, etc. Note: For any source it is always important to carefully check the appropriateness of the materials.

Procedure

1. Show a funny, incongruent picture to the students.
2. Model surprise and joy, and explain in detail what is funny about the picture.
3. Ask the students to look at funny pictures or cartoons.
4. After modeling the expression of humor several times, ask the students to identify what is funny about the pictures or cartoons. Keep modeling by smiling and laughing as a response for the incongruency.

Evaluation

Evaluate the students using the Evaluation Form for Humor Activities (page 115) and Scoring Rubric (page 116). The teacher can also document the ability of the student to identify people, animals, or objects in the pictures, or comment and reflect back on the pictures.

ANIMAL SURPRISE!

Instructional format

Small group or classroom.

Learning objective

Participants will learn to enjoy humor and incongruency by engaging in silly, playful activities.

Potential content area application

Communication; language arts.

Materials

Plastic animal figurines or animal pictures (choose animals that the students are familiar with and know their sounds).

Procedure

1. Present the students with plastic animal figurines or pictures of animals.
2. Let each student choose an animal and hold it.
3. Ask the students to identify each animal.
4. Ask each student to imitate the animal (movement, sounds, etc.). Model imitation of the animal if necessary.

Modification

Using cut photographs or drawings, have the students try pairing a feature of one type of animal with another animal (a rabbit with a pig's noise), present it to the group and make funny sounds and movements of the new funny animal they created.

Evaluation

Evaluate the students using the Evaluation Form for Humor Activities (page 115) and Scoring Rubric (page 116). Teachers can also document the ability of the student to identify animals, and to put together different pieces of animals to create an original expression of humor.

SIMON SAYS

Instructional format

Small group.

Learning objective

Participants will learn to enjoy humor and incongruency by engaging in silly, playful activities.

Potential content area application

Communication; language arts; social skills; physical education and motor skills.

Materials

Chairs placed in a semicircle with one chair placed in front of the semicircle.

Procedure

1. Simon Says is a classic kids' game in which the leader, Simon, instructs others to do various actions. One child plays the role of 'Simon,' and he or she stands facing the crowd.

2. Simon (or the teacher) should explain to the others that Simon will give instructions to do various actions, and they must imitate the actions.

3. Simon (the game facilitator) then proceeds to say various commands (while demonstrating the action), such as, 'Simon says touch your head' or, 'Simon says wave your hand,' and so on.

4. Let each student have a turn being Simon.

5. Ask the students to share what they liked about the activity.

Modification

• For more advanced groups, explain to the students who are imitating Simon that Simon will give instructions that begin with 'Simon says,' and other times not. If the students imitate the action without Simon saying 'Simon says,' then the student is eliminated for that round. The goal is to only do something when Simon says so, and to do nothing when he doesn't.

• Add themes for the movements (such as animals, feelings, or sports).

Evaluation

Evaluate the students using the Evaluation Form for Humor Activities (page 115) and Scoring Rubric (page 116). Teachers can also document the ability of the students to come up with relevant movements and the ability to imitate others.

COMIC STRIPS
Instructional format
Small group.

Learning objective

Participants will learn to enjoy humor and incongruency by recognizing incongruency presented in pictures. Participants will learn to share humor with others in an appropriate way.

Potential content area application

Communication; language arts; math and science (sequencing).

Materials

Magazines or newspapers containing comic strips. Use comic strips with three or more pictures. Cut them to separate, mix, and put each cut strip into an envelope. Note: For any source it is always important to carefully check the appropriateness of the material. Some material may not be appropriate for children or to be presented in school.

Procedure

1. Explain to the students that they are going to participate in a fun activity using comic strips.

2. Show a funny comic strip to the students.

3. Model laughing and explain what is incongruent about the comic strip.

4. Give each student an envelope of cut comic strips and ask them to take out the pieces of the comic strip and put them in order.

5. Once they have put them in order, ask them to describe their funny comic strip to the other students. Encourage peers to give feedback letting each other know if the comic strip makes sense as sequenced. If it does not, the student should try again.

6. Once all the comic strips have been sequenced correctly, the students should work together to identify what is humorous about each comic strip.

Evaluation

Evaluate the students using the Evaluation Form for Humor Activities (page 115) and Scoring Rubric (page 116).

JOKE OF THE DAY

Instructional format

Individual or group setting.

Learning objective

Participants will learn to enjoy humor and incongruency by sharing humor appropriately with others.

Potential content area application

Communication; language arts; math and science.

Materials

Magazines, newspapers or a computer to access websites.

Procedure

1. Provide the students with magazines or newspapers, or a computer to access websites.

2. Ask each student to find two or three jokes that they like, and cut or print them.

3. Ask the students to share their jokes with the rest of the class.

4. Encourage the students to summarize how this activity made them feel, if they thought it was fun, and if they would like to do this activity again.

Evaluation

Evaluate the students using the Evaluation Form for Humor Activities (page 115) and Scoring Rubric (page 116). Teachers can also document the ability of the students to present the joke to others, and to respond appropriately to other jokes.

Table 8.1 Activities that promote self-efficacy

Name of activity	Description of activity	Approx. time of activity	Also related to: Optimism (O) Humor (H) Kindness (K) Resilience (R)	Potential content area application*
Being persistent	Using picture rehearsal scenes to cope with difficult assignments	5–8 minutes	O, R	C, L, S
Using an errorless learning technique	Using an errorless learning technique to learn a new task	5–20 minutes daily		C, L
Helping at home by doing things I am good at	Using task analysis to learn a new task and increase independence	30 minutes plus practice of skills	R	C, L, M, S, P
Teaching social initiation and play using video modeling	Using video modeling to encourage social initiation	10–20 minutes		C, L, S
Being a good rider on the bus	Acquiring appropriate behaviors by watching modeling	15–30 minutes	R	C, L, S, V
Developing self-efficacy in problem solving	Creating opportunities for students to ask for help when facing a problem	5–30 minutes	O, R	C, L, M, S
Overcoming challenges	Choosing a common challenge and performing it independently	Depends on the task	O, R	Depends on the task
Look what I did in art class	Preparing artwork for display	30 minutes	R	C, L, S
I set my goals!	Learning to set realistic goals and encouraging a sense of accomplishment	5 minutes before and after an assignment	R	C, M, S
Earning 'I can do it' badges	Earning recognition for mastering an activity	2–15 minutes	R	C, L, S
'I can do it' tree	An ongoing display of learned skills			L, V

*Communication (C); language arts (L); math and science (M); social skills (S); physical education and motor skills (P); vocational and community skills (V)

Chapter 8

Activities that Promote Self-Efficacy

Table 8.1 on the opposite page lists the self-efficacy activities described in this chapter in relation to the other four areas of positive psychology: optimism, humor, kindness, and resilience.

BEING PERSISTENT

Instructional format

Individual student or small group.

Learning objective

Participants will develop coping skills, self-control, and persistence while engaging in challenges, by using positive self-talk during a problem-solving process.

Potential content area application

Communication; language arts; social skills.

Materials

Cognitive picture rehearsal scenes adhered to index cards (see Figure 8.1 for an example). Cut and paste each scene onto index cards. Scenes can be presented using flashcard style, storybook style, left to right tabletop layout, or put into photo albums. The script can be written underneath or on the back of the picture. It is important that the student focuses on the picture.

Procedure

1. Create a picture rehearsal scene, or refer to *Coping with Stress through Picture Rehearsal: A How-To Manual for Working with Individuals with Autism and Developmental Disabilities* (Groden *et al.* 2002) for examples of picture rehearsal scenes. See also pages 134–135.

2. Sit across from or next to the student and establish attention.

3. Read each card, in order, to the student.

4. After the student hears the scene in its entirety, ask the student to repeat the scene. Based on the communication abilities of the student, the scene can be said word for word, or the student can 'fill in the blanks,' repeating key words or phrases when prompted by the teacher. This can be done orally or with sign language. If the student is non-verbal, read the scene twice with the student pointing to the pictures or turning the cards to indicate participation.

5. After the second reading, ask the student questions to gauge comprehension of the scene.

6. Give verbal or tangible reinforcements to the student for participating in the session.

7. Practice the scenes on a daily basis (when introducing new scenes, practice them two or three times each day).

8. Introduce familiar scenes before, during or after a challenging event is encountered.

9. Emphasize key phrases such as 'Everyone finds it hard to learn new things,' or 'Everyone makes mistakes,' during relevant activities to assist the student in using the skill functionally.

Modification

- Ask the student to recall events resembling the scene and how he or she feels about it.

- Discuss why situations described in the scene are fundamental to the learning process.

- Ask the student to suggest future events he or she expects to be challenging and how he or she plans to handle them.

Evaluation

- Write anecdotal notes on the student's attention and participation.

- Evaluate the student's ability to use the strategies in real-life situations.

USING AN ERRORLESS LEARNING TECHNIQUE

Instructional format

Individual student.

Learning objective

Participants will increase self-efficacy by learning a new task using an errorless learning strategy (gradually reducing visual, auditory, and physical prompts and directions until the student masters the skill). The errorless learning strategy helps to eliminate the frustration of failure.

Potential content area application

Communication; language arts.

Materials

Four placemats and one place setting (plate, glass, fork, knife, spoon). On three of the placemats, outline the areas where the plate, glass, and utensils should be placed. The outlines on the first placemat should be bold, slightly faded on the second placemat, slightly more faded on the third placemat, and the last placemat should be unmarked (see Figure 8.1 for an example).

Sample Picture Rehearsal Scene

1 'I am doing my work. I find a question that seems hard.'

2 'I take a deep breath and relax. I can think clearly.'

✓

3 'I read the problem carefully, think, and try my best to solve it.' (add A or B)

A   'I know the answer and write it down.

The teacher says it is correct.

I feel proud I did it myself. I can do things like this.'

B   'I raise my hand and ask for help.

I wait patiently until the teacher comes over to help me.

The teacher shows me how to solve the problem.

I do what the teacher says and write down the answer.

I feel proud I asked for help.'

4 'I did a great job with my work. Now I imagine that the teacher is proud of me!'

✓

Procedure

The student is provided with placemats outlining the appropriate locations for the place settings. The outlines gradually fade (see B, C, D in Figure 8.1) until the student is capable of setting the table with no outlines at all.

FULL PHYSICAL PROMPT WITH FULL VISUAL AND VERBAL PROMPT

1. Put the placemat with the boldest outline on the table. Place the plate, glass, and utensils to the side of the student.

2. Ask the student to pick up the plate and place it on the placemat.

3. Prompt the student by taking the student's hands, helping the student pick up the plate and place it correctly.

4. Reinforce the student with praise, 'You did it. You put the plate on the placemat. You can set the table. Good job!' Use edible reinforcers if needed.

5. Continue using full physical prompts with full visual and verbal prompts for the remaining items.

6. Continue for a few more trials until the student requires less support. Then proceed to next step using partial prompts.

PARTIAL PHYSICAL PROMPT AND PARTIAL VISUAL PROMPT

1. Put the slightly faded placemat on the table and ask the student to pick up the plate and put it on the placemat.

2. Lift the student's hand toward the plate but let go before completing the motion to see if the student finishes the skill correctly. If the student completes the motion, reinforce the student. If the student doesn't finish, help the student finish and reinforce. Continue in the same way for each item.

3. Proceed with several more trials, reinforcing those trials requiring the least amount of assistance with enthusiastic praise.

4. As less assistance is needed by the student, replace the second placemat with the third placemat (more faded outlines) and continue with the trials until the student is ready to proceed to the next step (no prompts).

NO PHYSICAL OR VISUAL PROMPT

1. Put the placemat without any outlines on the table.

2. Ask the student to pick up the plate and put it on the placemat.

3. The student should complete the action correctly. If not, go back to partial prompting for a few more trials. If the student completes the step, reinforce enthusiastically and repeat several times.

4. Continue for each item.

Note

- Always finish a session with a successful trial.

- In addition to teaching this skill within direct instruction sessions, practice this skill in natural settings to facilitate its functional use.

- Reinforcers should be selected based upon known preferences and the student's response.

- Verbal praise should incorporate language that supports self-efficacy. These statements should emphasize effort and achievement, for example, 'You are a hard worker,' or 'The more you practice, the better you get,' or 'You can set the table.'

- Quickly move from the scripted directions to more functional requests, such as 'Set the table, please,' and praise the fact that they are good at setting the table themselves.

Figure 8.1 An example of visual prompts in errorless learning

HELPING AT HOME BY DOING THINGS I AM GOOD AT

Instructional format

Individual student or small group.

Learning objective

Participants will increase their independence by learning to perform tasks using a task analysis strategy.

Potential content area application

Communication; language arts; math and science; social skills; physical education and motor skills.

Materials

Depends on tasks chosen by the students; Task Analysis Worksheets (see pages 140–143), each of which includes visual guidelines at the bottom of the page.

Procedure

1. Seat the students and ask them to generate a list of tasks that they can do in their home environment such as folding towels, unloading the dishwasher, making a salad, or sweeping the floor.

2. Write the tasks on the board and ask the students to identify which ones can be practiced at school. Cross out the activities that cannot be practiced at school.

3. Ask the students to each pick one task from the remaining list that they are interested in learning and write their name next to the task.

4. Break each task into small manageable steps and have the students practice each step until they are capable of performing the task independently. Praise the student, and encourage them to perform the task at home.

5. Inform the parents that their child has practiced a certain task at school so that the parents can encourage their child to perform the task at home.

Modification

Students with the ability to perform writing assignments can fill out the Helping At Home Worksheet (page 144).

Evaluation

Evaluate the activity using a Task Analysis Worksheet (pages 140–143).

The following Task Analysis Worksheets are designed to evaluate a child's task while helping at home. This will help to improve the child's self-efficacy in being good at helping around the house.

Folding Towels Task Analysis Worksheet

Date of trial					
Steps	**Type of prompt (see code)**				
1 Lay towel flat on table horizontally.					
2 Pick up both corners on the right, pull the corners to the left edge of towel to fold the towel in half, and release.					
3 Pick up both corners at the bottom, fold up to the top edge, and release.					
4 Pick up both corners of left side, fold over to meet the right edge of towel, and release.					
5 Pick up the towel.					
6 Place towel neatly in the closet.					
TOTAL NUMBER OF I'S					

Code: G = gestural prompt; V = verbal prompt; I = independent, no prompts

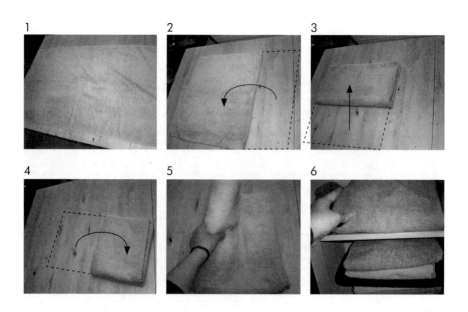

Unloading the Dishwasher Task Analysis Worksheet

Date of trial					
Steps	**Type of prompt (see code)**				
1 Open the dishwasher.					
2 Gently pull out one of the basket drawers.					
3 Pick up a cup.					
4 Put the cup on the shelf. Continue with all cups.					
5 Pick up a plate.					
6 Put the plate on the shelf. Continue with all plates.					
7 Put the utensils in their correct places in the kitchen drawer.					
8 When the dishwasher is empty, gently push the basket drawers into the dishwasher and close the door.					
TOTAL NUMBER OF I'S					

Code: G = gestural prompt; V = verbal prompt; I = independent, no prompts

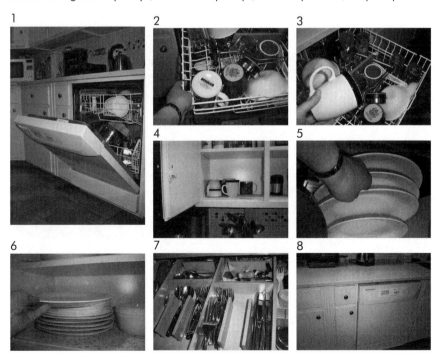

✓

Making a Salad Task Analysis Worksheet

(Hands should be washed before beginning this task.)

Date of trial					
Steps	**Type of prompt (see code)**				
1 Open the salad spinner.					
2 Take the lettuce and carrots out of the refrigerator.					
3 Shred the lettuce using fingers and place lettuce into the salad spinner.					
4 Rinse lettuce under water.					
5 Pour water into the sink.					
6 Spin the lettuce for 30 seconds.					
7 Transfer the lettuce into a bowl.					
8 Add pre-washed baby carrots.					
TOTAL NUMBER OF I'S					

Code: G = gestural prompt; V = verbal prompt; I = independent, no prompts

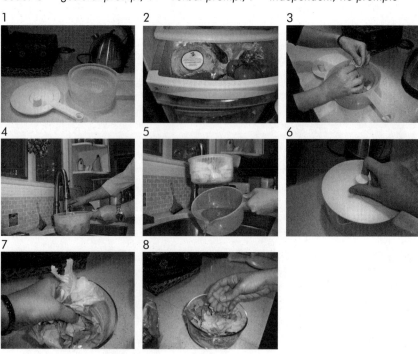

✓

Sweeping the Floor Task Analysis Worksheet

Date of trial					
Steps	**Type of prompt (see code)**				
1　Locate broom, dustpan, and trash container.					
2　Remove chairs and small items from area to be swept.					
3　Sweep dirt into a pile.					
4　Sweep dirt into a dustpan.					
5　Empty dustpan into trash container.					
6　Put away broom and dustpan.					
7　Replace chairs and small items.					
TOTAL NUMBER OF I'S					

Code: G = gestural prompt; V = verbal prompt; I = independent, no prompts

Helping at Home Worksheet

(Parents and students can complete this worksheet together.)

How can I help my family?

_____

_____

_____

_____

_____

What are three things I am good at and can do around the house?

_____

_____

_____

_____

What does my family say about my help?

_____

_____

_____

_____

✓

TEACHING SOCIAL INITIATION AND PLAY USING VIDEO MODELING

Instructional format

Individual student.

Learning objective

Participants will increase self-efficacy by learning to play using a video modeling strategy.

Potential content area application

Communication; language arts; social skills.

Materials

Three or four toys that the student has some familiarity with such as a ball, a musical toy, or a board game; a video camera; equipment for recording, editing, and viewing the video.

Procedure

1. Videotape a typically developing child approaching a peer or teacher while holding a toy and asking, 'Do you want to play?' The child waits for a positive response and then goes to play with the peer or teacher for about 15 seconds. The videotape should be about 30 seconds long. It is preferable to videotape individuals familiar to the student. For non-verbal students, gestures, sign language, or picture cards can be used to initiate the interaction.

2. Immediately prior to playtime, have the student watch the video.

3. Take the student to the play area with the same toys as depicted in the video.

4. Wait a few seconds for student to initiate play.

5. If the student initiates play, provide praise and reinforcement that includes playtime with the toy.

6. If the student does not initiate play, prompt with an expectant look.

7. If the student does not respond within a few seconds, model initiation of play for the student.

8. Repeat the procedure several times a day. As the student progresses, reduce the prompts and differentially reinforce independent initiation and shorter latency.

9. When initiation has been established, reinforce longer periods of play by choosing reinforcers that are natural to the activity.

10. Praise the child by saying, 'You are good at asking a friend to play.'

BEING A GOOD RIDER ON THE BUS

Instructional format

Small group.

Learning objective

Participants will develop self-efficacy in the area of bus riding behavior.

Potential content area application

Communication; language arts; social skills; vocational and community skills.

Materials

Index cards with smiley faces or 'Good Manners' written on them to hand to students.

Procedure

1. Position chairs in the classroom similar to seats on a bus.

2. Have the students board the imaginary bus and sit down.

3. Ask the students to model acceptable behaviors when riding on a bus (talking in a normal voice, staying seated, keeping hands relaxed, keeping feet on the floor).

4. Each time a student models good behavior, give them a Good Manners card.

5. Ask the students questions about various behaviors and if they are acceptable for riding on the bus ('Is it OK to run around on the bus?' etc.).

6. Praise and reinforce their recognition of good behavior.

Note: This format can be applied to teaching many tasks such as purchasing, going to the bank, going to a restaurant, and so on.

Modification

Allow the students to trade their Good Manners cards for reinforcers.

DEVELOPING SELF-EFFICACY IN PROBLEM SOLVING

Instructional format

Individual student.

Learning objective

Participants will develop self-efficacy skills by learning to identify a problem, find a solution and recognize the consequence. The importance of this activity is to teach the concepts of a problem and a solution, and associate the resulting outcome. By emphasizing the process, individuals who have difficulties or act out when faced with a problem learn to pursue a solution.

Potential content area application

Communication; language arts; math and science (sequencing); social skills.

Materials

Sequencing picture examples (Figure 8.2); problem solving evaluation table (Table 8.2).

Procedure

1. Focus on a problem that the student deals with on a regular basis and is motivated to solve, such as having dirty hands.

2. When the problem occurs, present a picture of the problem to the student and verbalize the problem in simple terms to help the student understand the problem.

3. Then show the student a picture of the solution (such as washing hands) and verbalize it for the student.

4. Finally, show the student a picture of the result (clean hands) and verbalize it for the student.

5. Have the student solve the problem (wash hands). Provide support if needed.

6. Review the sequencing pictures and the steps taken by pointing to the pictures and verbalizing the steps: 'In the beginning your hands were dirty, you washed your hands, and now your hands are clean.'

Modification

Provide multiple problems, solutions, and results and ask the student to sort and match them in correct sequence.

Evaluation

Use the problem solving evaluation table (Table 8.2).

Step 1 – presenting the problem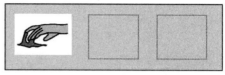

Step 2 – presenting the solution

Step 3 – presenting the result

Figure 8.2 Example of sequencing cards used for teaching a problem (dirty hands), the solution (washing hands), and the result (clean hands)

Source: The Picture Communication Symbols ©1981–2010 by DynaVox Mayer-Johnson LLC. All Rights Reserved Worldwide. Used with permission.

Table 8.2 Problem solving evaluation table

	Not yet capable	Capable with intensive support	Capable with some support	Capable with no support
Student identifies the problem card	1	2	3	4
Student identifies a solution card	1	2	3	4
Student can redirect self to perform the solution	1	2	3	4
The student identifies the consequence card	1	2	3	4

OVERCOMING CHALLENGES

Instructional format

Individual student.

Learning objective

Participants will develop self-efficacy in coping with challenges. In this activity, the focus is on performing tasks that the participants already know how to perform, but are slightly challenging. The challenge is to stay on task and develop self-control skills to complete the task with minimal reminders and redirections.

Potential content area application

Depends on the task: communication; language arts; math and science; social skills; physical education and motor skills; vocational and community skills.

Materials

Pictures of activities that the student already knows how to perform but are slightly challenging (Figure 8.3); poster board with 'I Did It' as the heading; materials depending on activity chosen; Overcoming Challenges Evaluation Form (page 152).

Procedure

1. Select pictures of activities that the student already knows how to perform but are slightly challenging.

2. Ask student to choose an activity from the selection.

3. Have the student complete the activity with minimal prompts. Provide encouragement when needed; redirect the student back to the activity if he or she becomes distracted.

4. After the activity, have the student place the picture of the activity on the 'I Did It' poster board.

5. Discuss with the student why it feels good to do tasks independently.

6. Reinforce the student for his or her work. Have the student say, 'If I can do this, I can _____' (have the student fill in the blank).

Modification

This activity can emphasize the area of kindness if the actions performed include kind behaviors.

Evaluation

Use the Overcoming Challenges Evaluation Form (page 152).

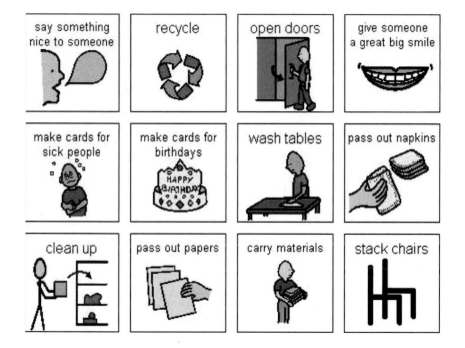

Figure 8.3 Examples of activity choices

Source: The Picture Communication Symbols ©1981–2010 by DynaVox Mayer-Johnson LLC. All Rights Reserved Worldwide. Used with permission.

Overcoming Challenges Evaluation Form

Date	Student	Task	Number of verbal redirections	Number of physical redirections	Comments

LOOK WHAT I DID IN ART CLASS

Instructional format

Small group.

Learning objective

Participants will increase self-efficacy by creating and presenting original art projects.

Potential content area application

Communication; language arts; social skills.

Materials

Display area; materials vary depending on art project.

Procedure

1. During art class, ask students to create individual artwork.
2. Display their artwork in an area in the classroom, or in a common area in the school.
3. Invite other staff or parents to visit and view the art projects.
4. Ask the students to talk about their artwork with visitors, present their artwork, answer questions, and so on.

I SET MY GOALS!

Instructional format

Individual student or small group.

Learning objective

Participants will develop coping skills, self-control, and persistence while engaging in challenges by following a process of setting goals and accomplishing them. Research shows that students who set their own goals achieve more than when goals are set for them by someone else. Setting their own goals will help students develop motivation and self-regulation and how to correctly assess the time required and complexity of the goal.

Potential content area application

Communication; math and science (time, number of assignments); social skills.

Materials

I Set My Goals Worksheet (page 155).

Procedure

1. Choose an assignment that the student can perform independently and that can be broken into units, such as reading a specific number of pages, solving a specific number of math problems, making a specific number of sandwiches (when working in a cafeteria), or folding a specific number of towels. If the student cannot visualize the number of items to be completed, use coins or other tokens to clarify the task length (bookmarks show number of pages to read, a box which just fits the prescribed number of sandwiches to be made, etc.).

2. Ask the student to fill in the I Set My Goals Worksheet indicating how many units of the activity the student plans to complete. If the student finds the decision difficult or chooses unrealistic goals (reading 100 pages in ten minutes), provide a realistic range to choose from (reading four, six, or eight pages in 15 minutes).

3. Have the student perform the activity independently. Praise the student upon achieving the goal. If the goal was not achieved, discuss what actions should be taken so that the student can achieve the goal.

I Set My Goals Worksheet

Name: _____

Date: _____

Today I will do:

_____

_____

_____

_____

I completed:

_____

_____

_____

_____

Please circle: I did it!   I will try again later!

✓

EARNING 'I CAN DO IT' BADGES

Instructional format

Individual or small group.

Learning objective

Participants will develop positive views about themselves by recognizing their own achievements.

Potential content area application

Communication; language arts; social skills.

Materials

Fabric or ribbon for sashes; badges or round stickers.

Procedure

1. Make a sash for each student and pin the sashes onto the bulletin board.

2. Ask each student to name a task or activity they have mastered. Ask the student to say, 'I can _____' Praise the student for each statement. Students with cognitive or language deficits can use sign language, gestures, facial expressions, or verbal approximations to express the statements.

3. Write the name of the task on a badge or sticker and adhere it to the sash.

4. On a daily basis, have the students practice 'I can' statements by using their badges on the bulletin board as a visual reference.

5. As the students master new skills, add a badge or sticker to their sash.

6. When appropriate, prompt students to show their sashes to visitors, peers, and school personnel.

'I CAN DO IT' TREE

Instructional format

Group.

Learning objective

Participants will develop self-efficacy by recognizing their own capabilities.

Potential content area application

Language arts; vocational and community skills.

Materials

Paper tree and paper leaves.

Procedure

1. Create a paper tree and display it on a bulletin board.

2. Throughout the year, to help students keep an ongoing list of skills they master, have them write it on a paper leaf, along with their name, and hang it on the tree for display. Students may choose to present to the class the new skill they learned.

3. Periodically point out the tree to the students and discuss the skills they have learned.

Modification

Create a paper train and add on cars as skills are learned, or use holiday themes throughout the year.

Table 9.1 Activities that promote kindness

Name of activity	Description of activity	Approx. time of activity	Also related to: Optimism (O) Humor (H) Self-Efficacy (SE) Resilience (R)	Potential content area application*
Identifying opportunities for performing kind acts I	Practicing kind behaviors while walking around the school	30–45 minutes		C, P
Identifying opportunities for performing kind acts II	Identifying opportunities to perform kind acts in real situations			C, L, S
The positive pyramid	Learning the meaning of kindness by labeling acts of kindness after an activity	15 minutes		C, L, S
Animal therapy	Learning to act kindly toward animals	30–45 minutes	SE	C, L, S, P
Giving baskets	Collecting food items to be donated to a local shelter	Throughout the week or month	SE	C, S, V
Passing the kindness pin	Earning recognition for performing kind acts	5 minutes per day for a week		C, S
Giving compliments	Complimenting peers using photos and symbols as prompts	5 minutes	O	C, L, S
Kindness tree	Describing and displaying kind deeds that have been performed	5 minutes per day, seasonal		C, L, S
Random acts of kindness	Learning to identify kind acts	30 minutes		C, L, S
Secret pal	Performing random kind acts for a selected person, and then revealing identity to recipient	5 minutes per day for a week		C, S

*Communication (C); language arts (L); math and science (M); social skills (S); physical education and motor skills (P); vocational and community skills (V)

Chapter 9

Activities that Promote Kindness

Table 9.1 on the opposite page lists the kindness activities described in this chapter in relation to the other four areas of positive psychology: optimism, humor, self-efficacy, and resilience.

IDENTIFYING OPPORTUNITIES FOR PERFORMING KIND ACTS I

Instructional format

Small group or class.

Learning objective

Participants will learn to recognize, label, and perform kind behaviors.

Potential content area application

Communication; physical education and motor skills.

Procedure

1. Plan an interactive walk around the school or in the neighborhood that will present opportunities for the students to practice acts of kindness, such as opening doors for others, delivering items to someone, picking up dropped items, and so on.

2. Enlist the help of other school personnel or family members as needed.

3. As students encounter an opportunity to demonstrate kindness, offer a verbal cue such as, 'Look, something dropped on the floor,' or 'Please open the door for Janet.'

4. After each encountered scenario, label the behavior as a kind act and praise the students.

5. Repeat this activity daily in different settings.

Note: The level of prompting and support can be based on the students' capabilities.

Evaluation

Evaluate independent functioning during the performances of kind acts.

IDENTIFYING OPPORTUNITIES FOR PERFORMING KIND ACTS II

Instructional format

Individual.

Learning objective

Participants will learn to express care for others by initiating kind acts independently.

Potential content area application

Communication; language arts; social skills.

Materials

Reinforcers (a favorite snack, stickers, etc.).

Procedure

1. During the course of the school day, point out opportunities for acts of kindness (e.g., 'There's no room to write on the blackboard,' or 'The printer seems to be out of paper.').

2. If students do not respond, ask them to perform the kind act (erasing the board, getting more paper for the printer).

3. Once they have performed the kind act, use a reinforcer to reward their kind behavior.

Modification

Document, or have the students document, a list of kind acts they have performed in their journals. Periodically review the list with the students.

Evaluation

Evaluate prompt levels required for students to recognize the opportunity to perform a kind act and completion of the kind act.

THE POSITIVE PYRAMID

Instructional format

Individual student or small group.

Learning objective

Participants will learn to recognize and label kind behavior.

Potential content area application

Communication; language arts; social skills.

Materials

Stickers; drawing of a pyramid.

Procedure

1. This lesson should occur immediately upon returning from an activity that was related to being helpful and kind to others, for example, getting supplies for someone at school, cleaning up the playground, or delivering meals to seniors in the community.

2. Ask each student in turn to state one good thing he or she did during the activity. Examples of responses are 'I helped to clean-up,' or 'I was polite,' or 'I sat quietly on the bus.'

3. Write down the kind act identified by the students onto stickers.

4. Ask the students to attach their stickers to the pyramid.

5. Review the stickers and label their behavior as kind acts.

Modification

This project can be focused on good deeds at home.

Evaluation

Record notes regarding student participation and project completion.

ANIMAL THERAPY

Instructional format

Individual or small group.

Learning objective

Participants will learn to act kindly toward animals.

Potential content area application

Communication; language arts; social skills; physical education and motor skills.

Precaution

This lesson is to be facilitated by a certified animal therapist with a therapy dog.

Materials

To be provided by the animal therapist.

Procedure

1. Introduce the animal therapist and dog.

2. The therapist should review a set of rules with the students on how to interact with the dog, such as how to be kind to the dog, use gentle hands, use a normal voice, and so on.

3. After reviewing the rules, the therapist can call upon willing students one at a time to interact with the dog. The therapist and student can decide what activity they would like to do such as pet the dog, feed treats to the dog, brush the dog's fur, etc. Note: Students can choose not to take a turn and just watch.

4. As a student is interacting with the dog and the other students are watching, the teacher should label the acts of kindness, such as, 'Look how nicely Joey is brushing the dog.'

5. After everyone has had their turn and the therapist and dog have left the classroom, ask the students to report how it made them feel when they did something kind for the dog.

GIVING BASKETS

Instructional format

Individual or small group.

Learning objective

Participants will learn to express care for others by recognizing kind deeds and becoming motivated to be recognized for being kind.

Potential content area application

Social skills; vocational and community skills.

Material

Baskets (or boxes) large enough to hold packaged food items donated by parents.

Procedure

1. Create a flyer explaining that the students are collecting canned or boxed food items to donate to a local food shelter.

2. Ask the students to participate in the collection and give them flyers to distribute to the other students in the school to take home to their parents.

3. When items are brought in, help the students place them in the basket. Reinforce the students for being kind (place a sticker on their shirt to acknowledge their contribution, etc.).

4. On a designated day, take a field trip with the students to the food shelter so that they can donate the items. Ask the staff at the food shelter to praise the students to help them realize that people appreciate their contribution and that they are helping others.

PASSING THE KINDNESS PIN

Instructional format

Small group.

Learning objective

Participants will learn to express care for others by participating in kind deeds.

Potential content area application

Communication; social skills.

Materials

A kindness pin with a picture of a smiley face, helping hands, and so on.

Procedure

1. Show the kindness pin to the students and tell them that anyone who does a kind deed gets to wear the pin.

2. At the end of each day, ask the student wearing the pin to point out another student who has done a kind deed and have him or her pass the pin to that student for the next day. If needed, assist the students in identifying kind deeds performed by other students.

3. Continue until everyone has had the opportunity to wear the pin.

Modification

An alternate closing activity is to pass the kindness pin on to someone outside the classroom or group.

GIVING COMPLIMENTS

Instructional format

Individual student or small group.

Learning objective

Participants will learn to give compliments.

Potential content area application

Communication; language arts; social skills.

Materials

A photograph of each student; poster board; a small box containing photos, icons, symbols, or words depicting positive characteristic traits (helping others to clean, sharing with others, being a good friend, being nice to others, being funny, etc.).

Procedure

1. During circle time, choose a student to be the focus of attention for the day (the order of students can be arranged alphabetically or by birth date).
2. Put a picture of the student onto the poster board.
3. Ask the other students each to choose an item from the box of positive character traits.
4. Once they have chosen a trait, ask them to express it in the form of a compliment and have them attach it to the poster.
5. At the end of the day, summarize for the student the many compliments that were given by the classmates.

Evaluation

Keep an anecdotal record of the student's ability to identify and state positive traits about others.

KINDNESS TREE

Instructional format

Small group.

Learning objective

Participants will learn to express care for others by participating in kind deeds.

Potential content area application

Communication; language arts; social skills.

Materials

A paper tree (or real tree branches held in a bucket); paper leaves (page 168); tape.

Procedure

1. Ask the students to help set the tree in a prominent area of the classroom.

2. Tell the students that the leaves stand for acts of kindness.

3. Ask the students to point out a kind deed being demonstrated by others or when they themselves participate in a kind deed.

4. Write the act of kindness on a leaf.

5. Help the students attach the leaf to the tree.

6. Summarize for the students the many leaves (acts of kindness) that are on the tree.

Modification

This activity can be adapted to seasonal themes such as colorful autumn leaves, snowflakes, hearts (Valentine's Day), raindrops, flowers, etc.

Leaves Template

RANDOM ACTS OF KINDNESS

Instructional format

Small group.

Learning objective

Participants will learn to identify what a kind act is. The stories in *Kids' Random Acts of Kindness* (Conari Press) were written by children. Many of them are simple to understand and provide a child's point of view and language that give them a special flare. However, since the idea of kindness is abstract, this activity better suits students with a high level of verbal understanding.

Potential content area application

Communication; language arts; social studies.

Materials

Kids' Random Acts of Kindness (Conari Press).

Procedure

1. Read a story from the book to the students.
2. Ask the students to discuss ways they can help someone they know.
3. Make a list of their ideas.
4. Post the list in the classroom.
5. Help the students decide how they can accomplish their ideas of helping others.
6. Revisit the list from time to time with the students to review their success in executing the kind deeds.

Modification

Have the students draw a picture of their random act of kindness if they cannot write.

SECRET PAL

Instructional format

Small or large groups.

Learning objective

Participants will learn to express care for others by initiating kind acts independently. This activity encourages participants to consider another's point of view; they will have the opportunity to see how happy a person can be when presented something specific to their liking. Recipients will enjoy the surprise of a token of kindness and will have fun guessing who is being kind to them.

Potential content area application

Communication; social skills.

Materials

Secret Pal Worksheet (page 171).

Procedure

1. Ask each student to select someone at school to whom they would like to extend a kind deed.

2. Next the students need to determine what acts of kindness they will anonymously share with their Secret Pal throughout the week, such as writing a note, making cookies or a favorite food, sending a card with a picture of a cute animal or favorite flower (use7 the Secret Pal Worksheet to help guide the students).

3. Each day, have the students participate in the Secret Pal program.

4. At the end of the week, have the students reveal their identity to their Secret Pals.

Secret Pal Worksheet

My Secret Pal's name is _____

Things my Secret Pal likes:

Sports _____

Food _____

Relaxing time _____

Television _____

What will make my Secret Pal happy? _____

My plan:

_____

_____

_____

_____

_____

✓

Table 10.1 Activities that promote resilience

Name of activity	Description of activity	Approx. time of activity	Also related to: Optimism (O) Humor (H) Self-Efficacy (SE) Kindness (K)	Potential content area application*
Coping effectively with challenges	Using picture rehearsal to cope with making mistakes, accepting changes, and learning new skills	5–8 minutes	O, SE	C, L
Problem solving basic challenges	Developing problem-solving skills	5–10 minutes	O, SE	C, L, P
Learning about preferences and being able to communicate likes and dislikes	Learning how to express preference of activities	30 minutes or more	SE	C, L, S, P
Asking for help from a peer	Learning to turn to peers for help when presented with a challenge	5–15 minutes	O, SE	C, L, S
My community	Identifying resources within a community	20 minutes or more	SE	C, L, S
My solution is…	Identifying solutions for common problems	5 minutes or more	SE	C, L, M, S
Using the telephone	Practicing various phone call scenarios	5 minutes or more	SE	C, L, S
Positive assertions to build self-esteem	Identifying and writing about positive traits	20 minutes or more	SE	C, L
Step-by-step problem-solving plan	Charting problems and solutions, and predicting outcomes	20 minutes or more	O, SE	C, L

*Communication (C); language arts (L); math and science (M); social skills (S); physical education and motor skills (P); vocational and community skills (V)

Chapter 10

Activities that Promote Resilience

Table 10.1 on the opposite page lists the resilience activities described in this chapter in relation to the other four areas of positive psychology: optimism, humor, self-efficacy, and kindness.

COPING EFFECTIVELY WITH CHALLENGES

Instructional format

Individual student or small group.

Learning objective

Participants will develop coping skills, self-control, and persistence while engaging in challenges by practicing cognitive restructuring toward:

- Mistakes and failures (page 176)
- Transitions (page 177)
- Changes (page 178)
- Learning new skills (page 179)
- Asking for help (specific and generic) (pages 180–181).

Potential content area application

Communication; language arts; social skills.

Materials

Imagery scenes glued onto index cards, each step of each sequence on one index card (pages 176–181); reinforcer. Cut and paste each scene onto index cards. Scenes can be presented using flashcard style, storybook style, left to right tabletop layout, or put into photo albums. Add a reinforcer to the last card. The script can be written underneath or on the back of the picture. It is important that the student focuses on the picture.

Procedure

1. Using one of the imagery scenes provided, sit across from or next to the student and establish attention. Assess that the student is calm and ready for instruction.

2. Read each card, in order, to the student.

3. Progress with presenting the imagery scenes until the script is finished. The last card ('Now I imagine…') is the reinforcing scene. This scene should be personalized to the child and it should be something they find pleasant or something that they really like.

4. After the student hears the scene in its entirety, ask the student to repeat the scene. Based on the communication abilities of the student, the scene can be said word for word, or the student can 'fill in the blanks,' repeating key words or phrases when prompted by the teacher. This can be done orally or with sign language. If the student is non-verbal, read the scene twice with the student pointing to the pictures or turning the cards to indicate participation.

5. After the second reading, ask the student questions to gauge comprehension of the scene.

6. Give verbal or tangible reinforcements to the student for participating in the session.

7. Practice the scenes on a daily basis (when introducing new scenes, practice them two or three times each day).

8. Introduce familiar scenes before, during, or after a challenging event is encountered.

9. Emphasize key phrases such as 'Everyone finds it hard to learn new things,' or 'Everyone makes mistakes,' during relevant activities to assist the student in using the skill functionally.

Modification

1. Ask the student if any of the imagined scenes occurred and what the student did.

2. Discuss why it is important to act appropriately in the situations described in the scenes.

3. Ask the student to suggest future events that he or she expects to be challenging and how the student plans to handle them (what to say, what to do).

Evaluation

• Write anecdotal notes on the student's attention and participation.

• Evaluate the student's ability to use the strategies described in the picture rehearsal scene in real situations.

PROBLEM SOLVING BASIC CHALLENGES

Instructional format
Individual student.

Learning objective
Participants will develop problem-solving skills by learning to ask for help when in need.

Potential content area application
Communication; language arts; physical education and motor skills.

Mistakes and Failures

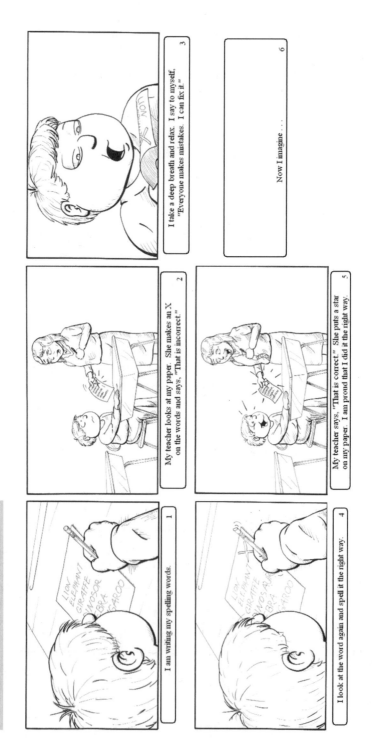

1. I am writing my spelling words.

2. My teacher looks at my paper. She makes an X on the words and says, "That is incorrect."

3. I take a deep breath and relax. I say to myself, "Everyone makes mistakes. I can fix it."

4. I look at the word again and spell it the right way.

5. My teacher says, "That is correct." She puts a star on my paper. I am proud that I did it the right way.

6. Now I imagine . . . .

Transitions

1 I am finishing up my reading program.

2 It is time to line up for gym.

3 I get in line. I don't have to be first.

4 I wait patiently and then walk with relaxed hands to the gym.

5 I am happy to be at the gym. What fun.

6 Now I imagine . . .

✓

Figure 10.1 Changes

Source: The Picture Communication Symbols © 1981–2010 by DynaVox Mayer-Johnson LLC. All Rights Reserved Worldwide. Used with permission.

Learning New Skills

1 I am in the classroom.

2 My teacher asks me to do something new that I have not done before.

3 I take a deep breath and relax. I know I can handle it. Trying new things is a great idea!

4 I say, 'Sure,' and do a good job learning the new activity.

5 Now I imagine . . .

Figure 10.2 Asking for help (specific)

Asking for Help (Generic)

1. I'm working on an activity that I don't know.

2. I take a deep breath and relax.

3. I hold up a card that says, 'Help.'

4. I get help, then I practice.

5. I can do it. I feel good.

6. Now I imagine . . . .

Materials

Problem Solving Basic Challenges Evaluation Form (page 184); other materials will depend on the problem presented.

Procedure

1. Choose an assignment or activity that the student cannot complete without asking for assistance. Examples of simple tasks are:

    o   ask student to perform a writing assignment, but do not offer a pencil

    o   offer a box of crayons that cannot be opened

    o   serve food items without appropriate utensils (i.e., soup with a fork)

    o   hand student an empty jug and ask him or her to fill cups with water

    o   ask student to retrieve an item from a locked cabinet

    o   ask student to get an item from a shelf too high for him or her to reach

    o   give student another student's personal item *as if by mistake.*

2. Give the student time to figure out that there is a problem.

3. If after a minute or two the student does not respond to the problem, ask the student if there is a problem.

4. If the student responds correctly, reinforce the student for recognizing the problem and for requesting help by providing positive responses such as, 'Good way of thinking about it!' (for realizing the problem), or 'Nice job asking for help!' (for asking for help), or 'What a great idea!' or 'You solved the problem!' (for searching for a solution or solving the problem).

5. If the student realizes that there is a problem but does not act on it (usually expressed by not responding, becoming frozen, getting upset, or walking away from the activity), provide hints or verbal/ visual cues to initiate action.

6. Alternatively, provide the solution immediately. For example, say, 'You need a teaspoon,' and ask the student to say 'I need a teaspoon' or sign or paint a picture of a teaspoon. Then give the student the teaspoon.

7. Continue with this activity multiple times until it is mastered.

Evaluation

Use the Problem Solving Basic Challenges Evaluation Form (page 184).

LEARNING ABOUT PREFERENCES AND BEING ABLE TO COMMUNICATE LIKES AND DISLIKES

Instructional format

Individual student or small group.

Learning objective

Individuals who are aware of their preferences are capable of advocating for themselves when being challenged. Learning how to pursue what brings one joy in the face of adversity increases the sense of well-being. Participants will increase their knowledge of self and become comfortable in expressing themselves.

Potential content area application

Communication; language arts; social skills; physical education and motor skills.

Materials

Picture cards of activities that the students are familiar with, sorted into categories (pages 186–188); a poster board divided into half with a happy face (Likes) on one side and a frown face (Dislikes) on the other side (see Figure 10.3 for a visual description of the procedure).

Problem Solving Basic Challenges Evaluation Form

Date							
Problem presented	**Result** 1 2 3 4	**Result** 1 2 3 4	**Result** 1 2 3 4	**Result** 1 2 3 4	**Result** 1 2 3 4	**Result** 1 2 3 4	**Result** 1 2 3 4
No pencil							
Unopened box							
Soup with fork							
Empty jug							
Locked cabinet							
Shelf too high							
Mismatched personal item							

1 = *Does not communicate about the problem and does not try to solve it*
2 = *Does not communicate about the problem but tries to solve it*
3 = *Communicates about the problem and/or asks for help*
4 = *Communicates about the problem and acts effectively to solve it*

✓

Procedure

1. Sort picture cards into categories such as leisure time, chores, physical activities, arts, and so on.

2. Present a category and the various activities within the category to the students.

3. Ask a student to choose an activity and decide where to place the picture of the activity (under Likes or Dislikes on the poster board). Provide assistance to ensure that the student understands and can express his or her actual thoughts and feelings about the activities. Present realistic opportunities so the student can express his or her preferences. Make sure the student is given a choice, and praise him or her for making a choice and carrying it out.

4. Repeat step 3 with all students in the group.

5. Ask students to discuss which of the activities they like and dislike.

Modification

Ask students to:

- use the cards to create a hierarchy of preferences
- choose between options and provide reasoning for their choices
- judge what activity is appropriate in different situations
- label the category of group of activities
- name items within a category.

Evaluation

Evaluate each student on their ability to express choices.

Samples of Categories to Choose From

LEISURE TIME

Computer

Reading a book

Making a puzzle

Listening to music

Reading a magazine

Watching TV

Play dough

Art

✓

CHORES

Emptying dishwasher

Sweeping

Putting away towels

Doing laundry

Gardening

Taking care of pets

Grocery shopping

✓

PHYSICAL ACTIVITIES

Swimming

Bicycling

Playground

Gym

COMMUNITY OUTING

Shopping

Library

Restaurant

Gym

Art class

1 The teacher explains the lesson and presents picture cards of various activities to the students

2 Student chooses her activity

3 Student decides where to place the picture of the activity (under Likes or Dislikes)

4 Repeat steps 2 and 3 with all students in the group

5 Teacher and students discuss the likes and dislikes of the group

Figure 10.3 Visual description of procedure

ASKING FOR HELP FROM A PEER

Instructional format

Individual student or small group.

Learning objective

Participants will develop problem-solving skills by learning to ask for help when in need. A key step in resilience is the ability to identify resources of support that can provide help when needed. In this activity, participants role-play how to help a peer, or how to get help from a peer. This activity increases their awareness of peers and empowers them as they see their peers and themselves act as role models. This activity can also be used to teach kindness given the different roles of the participants.

Potential content area application

Communication; language arts; social skills.

Materials

A picture card signifying help (if needed); materials to perform the selected assignment; Asking for Help Evaluation Form (page 192).

Procedure

1. Make a list of tasks that each student is familiar with and is capable of doing, and that can be done by two people. Examples of tasks include:

   ○ carrying items from one room to another or to the office

   ○ setting the table for a meal

   ○ cleaning up an area

   ○ locating an object or a person

   ○ packing a bag for a community outing

   ○ supporting a peer when distressed.

2. Assign a task to a student and designate a helper (a peer who knows how to perform the task).

3. Encourage the student to initiate the task and to ask for assistance from their assigned helper, as needed.

4. Shadow the student and helper as they perform the task.

5. Reinforce appropriate request for help by the student.

6. Reinforce the helper for showing kindness.

Evaluation

Use the Asking for Help Evaluation Form (page 192) to evaluate each student's participation based on his or her:

- understanding of the scenario
- request for assistance
- use of the skill in real-life situations.

MY COMMUNITY

Instructional format

Individual student or small group.

Learning objective

Participants will develop problem-solving skills by identifying services and resources in the class, school, and the community that can help them solve various problems.

Potential content area application

Communication; language arts; social skills.

Materials

Pictures or symbols of school or places in the community (page 194); My Community Evaluation Form (page 195).

Asking for Help Evaluation Form

Student's name	Assignment	Helper's name	Asking rating	Time of working cooperatively with the helper	Task completed successfully?

Evaluation rating:
1 = Requires intense physical and verbal support to ask for help/work cooperatively
2 = Requires some physical and/or verbal support to ask for help/work cooperatively
3 = Needs additional verbal directions to ask for help/work cooperatively
4 = Asks for help/works cooperatively with no support from teacher

Procedure

1. Present pictures or symbols to students, one at a time, and discuss briefly the function of each person or place.

2. Ask students questions that will require them to solve a problem. Examples of questions are:

   At school:

   o   Your hands are dirty. What should you do?

   o   Who helps you when you are sick?

   o   Where do you go to copy papers?

   o   If you can't find your lunch box, who can help you?

   In the community:

   o   Where do you go to buy food?

   o   Where would you go out to eat?

   o   Who helps to put out a fire?

3. Use the pictures or symbols to prompt the students to the correct answer, if needed. Praise the students for their correct answers.

Modification

- Use indirect questions that require deduction such as, 'There is no food at home. What do you do?' (go to the supermarket), or 'There is no copy paper left. What do you do?' (go to the office).

- Ask practical questions without using the pictures and symbols, for example, 'You've come home from school and have no keys. What do you do?' or 'You didn't get off at the right bus stop. What do you do?'

Evaluation

The teacher can document the questions, prompts, and answers in the My Community Evaluation Form (page 195).

Symbols of School and Community

Nurse

School office

Water cooler

Washing hands

Lockers

Classroom

School

Hospital

Gas station

Doctor

My Community Evaluation Form

Name	Question asked	Response
e.g., John	Who helps you when you are sick?	The doctor
e.g., Emma	Where do you put your jacket?	The locker

✓

MY SOLUTION IS . . .

Instructional format

Individual or two students.

Learning objective

Participants will develop problem-solving skills by identifying various solutions to problems.

Potential content area application

Communication; language arts; math and science; social skills.

Materials

Ladder Board (page 197); two different colored game pieces; index cards with questions that require three answers, or one answer with three steps.

Procedure

1. Seat two students in front of the Ladder Board.

2. Assign a game piece and a ladder to each student.

3. In turn, ask each student to pick up a card and read the question.

4. Ask the student to think of an answer to the question. If he or she provides a correct answer, have the student move his or her game piece up the ladder, and then ask the other student a question. If the student is unable to think of a response or gives an incorrect response, the turn passes to the other student.

5. When one of the students has provided three answers, they should be given a prize (a primary reinforcement such as candy, or a secondary reinforcement such as a sticker or a coin). Continue to do this for the duration of the game. If using stickers or coins, the student who earns the most is considered the winner.

Examples of questions for the cards:

- What are three things you should wear when it's raining?

- What are three things you can wear if it's very cold?

Ladder Board

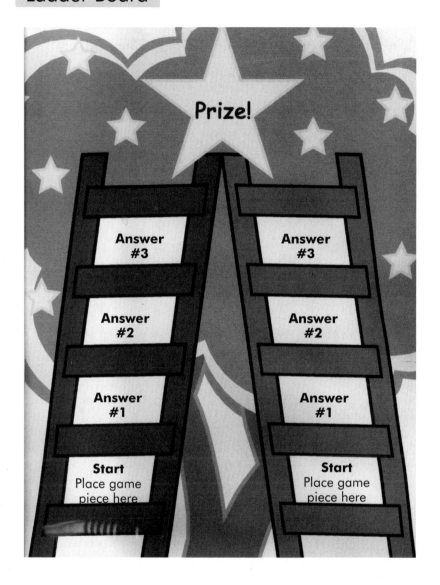

- What are three gifts you can give a friend for a birthday?
- Which three people can you talk to when you don't feel well?
- Which three people can you ask for help if you don't know how to do your work?
- What can you do if the electricity goes out?
- What can you do if it is too noisy?
- What can you do if you can't fall a sleep?
- What can you do if you do not understand a question in your homework?
- How do you make a sandwich?
- What do you do if you are bullied?
- What do you do if you hurt someone's feelings?
- What do you do if your friend is playing on the computer and you want to play too?
- What do you do if you are lost?
- What do you do if you meet a person that you don't know?
- What do you do when you have an incorrect answer on your schoolwork?
- What can you do if your parents ask you to do a chore that you do not like?
- What can you do if you are offered new food that you are not familiar with?
- What can you do while you wait in line?
- What can you do if someone is crying?

USING THE TELEPHONE

Instructional format

One or two students.

Learning objective

Participants will develop problem-solving skills by using an important tool, the telephone. A key skill in being resilient is using the telephone to meet everyday challenges.

Potential content area application

Communication; language arts; social skills.

Materials

Scripts for phone conversations (pages 200–201); two unconnected phones (optional); Using the telephone evaluation table (Table 10.2).

Procedure

1. Choose a phone conversation for the student to learn (calling the emergency services if someone is hurt, ordering a pizza, calling a friend to invite him or her over to the house to play, or calling the library to check their hours).

2. Present the appropriate script to the student and help the student fill out the missing details (phone number, friend's name, etc.).

3. Have the student pretend to make the phone call, using the script to navigate through the phone call.

4. Have the student practice the script a few times, changing the script as needed.

5. Ask a second student to participate as the person answering the phone call and guide both students through the role-play session.

Modification

- Change the script and make the conversation more complex. For example, the student can ask what time the pizza will arrive, how much it will cost, or add drinks to the order.

- Have the student perform a real phone call with guidance and supervision.

Calling Emergency Services Script

Dial emergency services number (e.g., 911 in the USA or 999 in the UK)

(Wait to hear a person answer)

Ask: 'Is this 911?' (or appropriate number)

(Wait to hear if the person says yes)

Say: 'My name is _____

_____ is hurt and needs help

My address is _____

_____

Please come quickly!'

Don't hang up the phone.

Stay on the line and listen to directions.

Ordering Pizza Script

Dial: _____

(Wait to hear a person answer)

Ask: 'Is this _____?' (Name of pizza place)

(Wait to hear answer)

Say: 'I would like to order ____(how many)_____(size) pizza(s)
with_____ (toppings), please'

(Wait to hear answer)

Say: 'My address is:_____

_____,

(Listen to answer)

Say: 'Thank you!'

Hang up the phone.

✓

Inviting a Friend to Your House to Play Script

Dial your friend's phone number: _____

    (Wait to hear a person answer)

Say: 'Can I speak with _____ please?'

    (Listen to the answer)

When your friend answers

Say: 'Hello _____, this is _____

    Would you like to come over and play today at _____(time)?'

    (Listen to the answer)

If your friend says 'Yes'

Say: 'OK, see you then, bye!' and hang up the phone.

OR

If your friend says 'I am sorry but I can't come today'

Say: 'That's OK, we can try another time!'

    (Listen to the answer)

Then say: 'Goodbye.'

At the end of the conversation, hang up the phone.

Calling the Library Script

Place a notepad and pen next to the phone.

Dial your library's phone number: _____

    (Wait to hear a person answer)

Say: 'Hello, is this the library?'

    (Listen to the answer)

Ask: 'What are your hours today?'

    (Write down the answer on the notepad)

Say: 'Thank you!

At the end of the conversation, hang up the phone.

✓

Evaluation

- Document the success of the phone conversation by selecting the appropriate number from Table 10.2.
- The phone conversations can be taped and kept for documentation.

Table 10.2 Using the telephone evaluation table

1	2	3	4	5	6
The student requires intense support reading the text or following the visual cues to follow the text	The student can read the text or follow the visual cues with some support and reminders	The student follows the text and visual cues easily, however is not flexible if the conversation extends beyond the text	The student does not require a written script at all, however is not flexible if the conversation extends beyond the text	The student does not require a written script at all and is flexible if the conversation needs to extend beyond the text	The student generalizes skills to real-life situations
Evaluate the student's capacity to converse using the scripts provided.					

POSITIVE ASSERTIONS TO BUILD SELF-ESTEEM

Instructional format

Individual or small group.

Learning objective

Participants will develop a positive view about themselves by assigning positive attributes to themselves. Knowing one's strengths contributes to being resilient because when faced with challenges, people are more likely to be proactive if they feel confident.

Potential content area application

Communication; language arts.

Materials

My Strengths Worksheet (page 205); reinforcers; a binder (optional).

Procedure

1. Assist the student in identifying something he or she did well during the day, or in which he or she showed positive characteristics. Do this by recalling situations and communicating them, such as 'It was kind of you to share your books with Danielle during recess today.'

2. Have the student write the behavior on the My Strengths Worksheet (page 205).

3. Help the student identify positive traits associated with the behavior listed, for example, 'I am a sharing person.'

4. Encourage the student to add positive and encouraging text such as, 'I can do new things!' or, 'I can handle it!' or, 'My teacher is very proud of me.'

5. Provide social or tangible reinforcers for the behavior, such as food, stickers, activities, or privileged responsibilities at schools.

6. Let students share their worksheets by reading them at group or circle time. Encourage the students to talk about events represented in the worksheet and about their strengths.

7. Ask other students to show their appreciation for their friend's accomplishments. Teach this through demonstration and modeling of appropriate responses. These can include praise, clapping, high fives, writing a thank you note, drawing a picture, etc.

Tip for success: Remember that all accomplishments, whether seemingly small (learning to button a coat) or large (artwork displayed in an art exhibition), can be recognized and celebrated in this activity.

Modification

- For students with significant speech/language challenges, modify the procedure by using photographs, picture symbols, or other non-verbal communication strategies.

- The teacher can write the comments for students who are unable to do so.

- Ask the students how they feel about their positive behaviors or achievements.

- Encourage students to suggest additional acts they think are worthy of a compliment. Do this to determine what the student thinks is most important or is most proud of.

Evaluation

Keep a binder for each student and have them review it at designated times.

My Strengths Worksheet

My Strengths

What I did (behavior):

Example: I shared my books with Danielle during recess

_____

_____

_____

_____

_____

This shows that I...(attribute)

Example: I am a sharing person

_____

_____

_____

_____

_____

I feel good about myself!

✓

STEP-BY-STEP PROBLEM-SOLVING PLAN

Instructional format

Individual or two students.

Learning objective

Participants will develop problem-solving skills by following a plan to solve problems by breaking them down into small, manageable steps.

Potential content area application

Communication; language arts.

Material

Step-by-Step Problem-Solving Plan (page 208); Problem Solving Evaluation Form (page 209).

Procedure

1. Identify a problem for the student to solve. Choose a situation that has occurred in the classroom, or use the samples provided below (common social problems in the classroom).

2. Describe the problem by telling a short story or by role-playing with another teacher.

3. Use the Step-by-Step Problem-Solving Plan to guide the student through the problem-solving steps.

4. What is the problem? Help the student state the problem in his or her own words. For some students it will be better to narrow the problem down to be more specific.

5. What can I do about it? Help the student generate strategies to resolve the problem. Not all the strategies need to be realistic. Expression of unrealistic ideas can be an opportunity to teach logical thinking and good judgment. Help the student break the solutions into small steps. For example, if the student is being pulled by another student and the solution is to respond assertively, help the student write in the Plan:

- ○ 'I call my teacher's name loudly.'
- ○ I say, 'Help me.'
- ○ I tell Jack, 'Stop pulling! I don't like it.'

6. What will happen next? Help the student imagine the expected outcome of each idea. Support the student in using critical thinking to figure out which idea is good and which idea is not good.

Modification

- Role-play specific scenarios with corresponding problem-solving strategies.
- Prompt the student to use his or her strategy in real-life situations.

Evaluation

Use the Problem Solving Evaluation Form (page 209) to evaluate the student's responses by ticking the appropriate boxes. Evaluation can also be based on the student's use of the skill in real-life situations.

COMMON SOCIAL PROBLEMS IN THE CLASSROOM

- Having a hard time responding appropriately to 'No.'
- Being delayed or prevented from doing a preferred activity.
- Being required to do a non-preferred activity.
- Being limited in food choices, or trying to implement dietary restrictions (classroom, home, restaurant).
- Waiting to take turns (game time, circle time).
- Disagreements with peers and friends on what activity to do.
- Being upset with sensory issues in the environment.
- Functioning in an unfamiliar social setting.
- Difficulty working with different teachers or peers.
- Fear of unfamiliar people.
- Difficulty overcoming disappointments (such as a planned trip to the swimming pool being cancelled).
- Learning how to handle bullies.

Step-by-Step Problem-Solving Plan

What is the problem?

What can I do about it?

1	2

What will happen next?

Problem Solving Evaluation Form

	Not yet capable	Capable with intensive support	Capable with some support	Capable with no support
Student understands the problem described to him or her, as expressed verbally or in writing				
Student can identify a solution to the problem				
Student can identify an alternative solution to the problem presented				
Student expresses logical decision making				
Student lays out steps for problem solving				
Student can role-play the solution				

✓

Chapter 11

But Wait, There's More

A Photography Program Pulls It All Together

Figure 11.1 Students in the Groden Center photography program

My Own World, the Groden Center's photography program, provides us with an example of how building 'islands of competence' can improve resilience as well as other positive psychology traits. Figure 11.1 shows students excited about photography. This chapter will discuss the project and its implementation and outcomes for children and adults with autism aged from 9 to 50. It will also focus on nurturing special capabilities in individuals with autism to increase resilience.

Art is a wonderful medium in which positive psychology related skills can be nurtured and practiced. Art lessons are often provided in a less structured environment as compared to other academic lessons, providing ample opportunities for incidental teaching of positive psychology themes. For example, students can be cued to find opportunities to act kindly by sharing art tools with their peers or by offering to assist them in cleaning up at the end of class. In addition, art can provide alternative expressive outlets for one's thoughts and emotions which helps a person feel connected and supported. For example, students can create gifts for others and express emotions such as love, anger, or joy.

The most exciting element of the arts for individuals with developmental disabilities is that art lessons often expose overlooked areas of strength or islands of competence. Islands of competence are hidden capabilities that are not regularly observed by the individual or by others (Brooks 1999; Brooks and Goldstein 2001). Expressing these capabilities provides the individual with a sense of self-worth and self-expression, and a feeling of being appreciated by others. Being identified as successful in any art field can negate the harmful effect of emotional threats such as facing social difficulties or academic failures.

MY OWN WORLD PROJECT GOALS AND DESCRIPTION

The My Own World program combines the philosophy of positive psychology with photography. The programs that develop positive psychology traits through the arts were rarely applied to individuals with autism. The photography lessons are designed for individuals with autism and include different themes that foster resilience and other characteristics within positive psychology. Photography is an excellent medium, allowing individuals with autism to excel since it is based on visual capabilities, a relative strength for many individuals with autism. In addition, photography requires only minimal fine motor skills and provides instant results that help to link effort with success, a feeling that is not experienced often by individuals with developmental disabilities. The behavioral-based curriculum is suitable for the whole spectrum of individuals with autism. Given the structured nature of the program, we put an emphasis on maintaining the students' freedom of artistic expression. Art exhibitions were included as part of the project. Displaying our students' artwork to the public increased awareness and appreciation of the capabilities of individuals with autism. It also increased the students' feeling of self-worth and provided them with an opportunity to contribute to the community.

About 100 children and adults at the Groden Center participate in this program each year. The age range of the students is 9–50 years old, and the students have various levels of cognitive challenges. At the beginning of the project the school staff members were presented with the project goals and philosophy. Before each lesson the staff members were provided directions by the photography instructor or art teacher. The lessons took place in classrooms, the art center, on field trips, and outdoor school areas. Each class consisted of between three and ten students, one to three students were assigned to one staff member (either a teacher or a teacher aide), and everyone was supervised by the photography instructor.

The cameras we used have a large screen view finder that produces professional quality photographs. The large view finder is crucial as it captures the students' attention and provides an easy way to focus using both eyes rather than closing one eye and focusing with the other. The cameras have their own photo print dock independent of a computer. We used desktop computers with photo processing programs, and photo printers, some with a professional large format photo printer. Using printing docks eased the process of printing and required minimal skill by pushing a button. A task analysis guide was developed for use with a computer-attached printer (how to feed the paper, check ink levels, etc.).

The photography project was set around five themes all designed to increase student awareness:

- Things I Like (relationships with the inanimate world).
- Friends (relationships with peers).
- Me (the individual's understanding of self).
- People I Love (relationships within the family).
- Celebrating Nature (relationships with nature).

The students learned to describe their photographs verbally and in writing as part of the language arts/communication curriculum. The students were asked to photograph landscapes, objects, or individuals according to the theme. They were also free to take photographs without instruction to allow for free expression. The staff members were directed to support but not intervene with the actual aiming of the camera. If aiming or shooting by the staff members was used for modeling, the photographs were then deleted.

Several lesson plans were developed for each theme to help students generalize the concepts learned. For example, the Things I Like theme focused on teaching students how to express their preferences and become a better self-advocate, and therefore more resilient. Studies done with individuals with developmental disabilities revealed they have significantly fewer opportunities for making choices, less autonomy, and less decision making regarding managing their free time compared to the general population (Sheppard-Jones, Prout and Kleinert 2005). The photography lessons in this theme were aimed at developing technical proficiency with the camera, while at the same time applying concepts of choice making. The students were asked to take photographs of things they like in the natural world, in an urban setting, or at school. Next, they were asked to make choices regarding their photographs such as what they would like to print, what to crop, and so on. The choices involved the understanding and discrimination between likes and dislikes. Therefore, as a first step, a lesson plan was developed to help students to express their likes and dislikes by sorting photographs of food items, leisure activities, chores, and other free time activities into those categories. Only after teaching the concept of likes and dislikes were the students presented with the printing and editing assignments.

The photography lessons were broken down into small steps and these steps were evaluated. The teachers recorded the students' independence in the task of asking for the camera, placing a strap around their neck, aiming the camera, taking the photographs and sharing the camera with others. After printing their photographs, the students filled out a record with their teachers. The purpose of this step was to help students link their efforts with successful results. The staff and photography teacher also used a task analysis (Figure 11.2) to teach and evaluate the process of other skills learned such as using editing photographs, matting, framing, presenting their artwork in exhibitions. Staff members provided positive feedback and encouragement and helped the students appreciate their achievements and progress which helped to increase their self-efficacy and resilience.

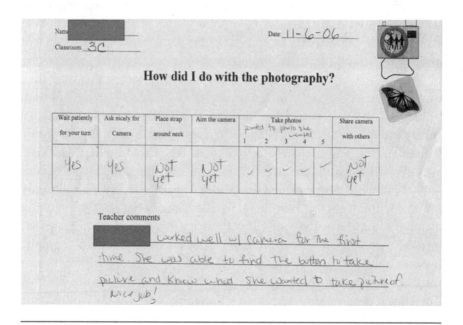

Name: _____ Date: 11-6-06

Classroom: 3C _____

How did I do with the photography?

Wait patiently for your turn	Ask nicely for Camera	Place strap around neck	Aim the camera	Take photos pointed to photo she wanted 1 2 3 4 5					Share camera with others
Yes	Yes	Not yet	Not yet	✓	✓	✓	✓	✓	Not yet

Teacher comments

_____ worked well w/ camera for the first time. She was able to find the button to take picture and knew what she wanted to take picture of. Nice job!

Figure 11.2 This chart breaks down a new skill (photography) into small manageable steps. This student did not do all the parts of the activity correctly or independently. However, she mastered some of them. While filling in the details with the teacher's help and with careful analysis, the student realized her accomplishment

The staff members communicated with parents about the skills, activities, and the pictures that were taken by sending home newsletters and by creating special shared projects at home and school. Parents were also invited to the exhibitions. The students attended the opening nights at the exhibitions, and learned to describe their pictures to others. Our student photographers (who usually find it difficult to be in public events) and their parents showed extreme pride and happiness when they saw their artwork on display along with their portrait and biography, and when presented with trophies and certificates.

For individuals with autism who often struggle with communication, photography provides a new means of self-expression to show how they view their world. With their cameras, students capture light, color, shapes, textures, reflections, landscapes, objects, and structures in the world around them. Those who are more capable also share ideas, humor, and special interests through photography. To view photographs and receive more information about the project, go to the Groden Center website at www.grodencenter.org/groden-center/myownworld.

Most of the students were very interested in participating in the photography classes. After some practice, about 80 percent of the photographs seem to be aimed purposefully. The students' photographs showed us what they perceived as interesting or important. Since the students were given only general directions regarding the content expected, their photographs represented their insights. Analysis of their photographic contents found no common idiosyncrasies, as has been documented in children with various kinds of disabilities (Dyches *et al.* 2004). However, we found that some students held specific interests. One of the students, a 37-year-old male with autism, was interested in photographing cylinders, poles, and street lamps. A student with Down's syndrome and hearing impairment mainly focused on photographing trees (see Figure 11.3). A 20-year-old student with autism was interested in naturally created geometric shapes and patterns (see Figure 11.4). A 16-year-old non-verbal student expressed humor and created illusions in his photographs (see Figure 11.5).

Figure 11.3 A photograph from a student who focuses on tree

Figure 11.4 A photograph from a student who focuses on geometric shapes and patterns

Figure 11.5 A non-verbal student in the photography program expresses humor and creates illusions in his photographs. In a series of photographs in a graveyard, he took photographs of tombstones with the last names of 'graves' and 'still' on them. He also photographed headstones from an angle that provides the illusion that they are skyscrapers

One of the obstacles in understanding the ideas expressed in the photographs was the deficit of verbal expression of students with autism and developmental disabilities. For example, Sylvia is an 18-year-old woman with autism whose language is limited to one- or two-word sentences. Sylvia is capable of capturing the whole object of her attention in her photographs. Therefore, the photography instructor was surprised to find that in the My Friends assignment Sylvia captured only half of the face of her favorite teacher. During the project, descriptions of the photographs were documented using journals (Figure 11.6) which were written either by the student or the teacher who elicited a description from the student where possible.

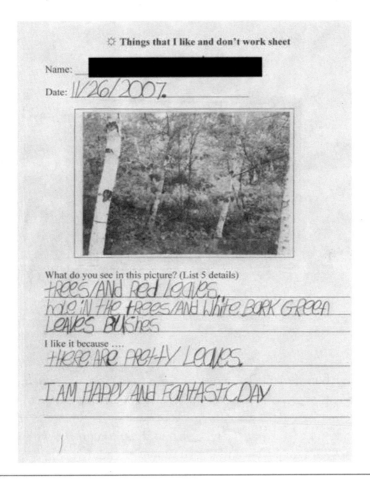

Figure 11.6 An example of a student's journal

During the journal assignment, Sylvia described her focus in the picture by saying the name of the teacher and the word 'pen.' Until that point the pen that the teacher kept on his ear seemed to be irrelevant to us. However, since Sylvia labeled it, and since the pen is located in the center of the photograph, we believe Sylvia was actually aiming at the pen as the focus of her interest. The journaling step is crucial to understanding the photographs and this step taught us that the students' focus of attention is different than what is expected. For example, we learned that the lamp in front of the building in Figure 11.7 is the subject of the photograph and not the State House building itself. Having the students describe their photographs provides us with the true message of the photographs.

Figure 11.7 The lamp in front of the building is the subject of the photograph and not the State House building itself

Presenting our students' photographs in art exhibitions increased their sense of mastery and achievement. They also felt that they contributed to the community. The students' photographs are an immense source of pride for many of our parents who shared the photographs with relatives and friends, and they were enthusiastic about attending exhibitions where their children's artwork was praised and purchased by individuals in the community. Since the project started, the students' photography work has been presented at the Autism Society of America's (ASA) annual meeting, Rhode Island Spring Flower and Garden shows, at City Hall in Providence, RI, and at Wheaton College in Norton, MA. The photographs were also presented at numerous exhibitions and holiday art sales within the Rhode Island area. At the exhibitions, students presented their photographs and if possible discussed their work with individuals from the community. The photographs are for sale and the students earn the money from the pictures that are sold and from the note cards in which they are reproduced. While allowing students to discover their own potential and then revealing those capabilities to their parents and to the community, we hope to contribute more to the well-being of our students and their parents and thereby help to increase their resilience and self-efficacy.

BUILDING AN ISLAND OF COMPETENCE WITH PHOTOGRAPHY

Table 11.1 Photography activities

Name of activity	Activity level	Approx. time of activity	Computer needed?
Indoor photography	Basic	45 minutes	
Outdoor photography	Basic	1–2 hours	
Scavenger hunt	Intermediate	1–2 hours	
Uploading and printing	Advanced	45 minutes	Yes
Photography and coloring	Advanced	1 hour or more	Yes
Connection to current events	Basic	45 minutes	Yes
Photography-related computer skills	Intermediate	45 minutes	Yes

INDOOR PHOTOGRAPHY (BASIC ACTIVITY)

Instructional format

Individual student or small group.

Learning objective

Participants will develop their island of competence by learning to use the camera to take pictures.

Materials

Digital camera and tripod.

Procedure

1. Ask the student to choose an item to photograph and place the item on a desk or table.

2. Have the student sit on a chair facing the camera viewer and look at the item through the viewer.

3. Prompt the student to press the button to take a photo of the item.

4. Review the image on the camera with the student and praise the student.

5. Discuss with the student how to change the angle of the photo, how to zoom in and out, and so on.

Figure 11.8 Students at the Groden Center taking pictures

OUTDOOR PHOTOGRAPHY (BASIC ACTIVITY)

Instructional format

Individual student or small group.

Learning objective

This activity teaches the basic skills of photography.

Materials

Digital camera with view finder.

Procedure

1. Explain to the students that they will be taking a field trip to an outdoor location to take pictures.

2. Choose a popular outdoor setting, one that the students will be excited to go to (a neighborhood park, the school playground, etc.).

3. Once at the location, ask the students to look around and identify items they would like to take pictures of.

4. Assist the first student in using the camera appropriately.

5. Have the student take pictures of one or several items, suggesting different angles, zooming in or out, and so on.

6. As each picture is taken, show it to the student on the picture viewer and offer praise.

7. Continue until all students have a turn taking photos.

Evaluation

• Use the Evaluation Form (Teacher Version) (page 222) to record the students' progress.

• Fill out the Evaluation Form (Student Version) (page 223) with the student. Write a tick in the appropriate column.

Evaluation Form (Teacher Version)

Date: _____ Classroom: _____

Location:_____

Name	Asking for the camera	Placing strap around neck	Aiming the camera	Taking photos	Sharing with others

Prompt hierarchy:
1 = Not doing it yet
2 = Full physical support
3 = Partial physical support
4 = With verbal support
5 = Independent

✓

Evaluation Form (Student Version)

How did I do with taking photographs?

Waited patiently for my turn	Asked nicely for the camera	Placed strap around neck	Took photographs	Shared camera with others

How did I do with printing?

Waited patiently for my turn	Placed camera on dock	Chose a photograph	Printed the photograph

✓

SCAVENGER HUNT (INTERMEDIATE ACTIVITY)

Instructional format

Individual student or small group.

Learning objective

In this activity, participants use their skills with the camera and apply them to a scavenger hunt game.

Materials

Digital camera with view finder; printer

Procedure

1. Create a list of items that students can find either in their own classroom or out in the community, such as:

    ○ items in specific colors or shapes, animals, letters, signs, items related to seasons

    ○ places in the school building

    ○ teachers and peers (to help students connect names to faces)

    ○ holiday-related items.

2. Take students to the designated area, provide them with the list and tell them they need to find the items on the list and take one photograph of each item.

3. When all items on the list are found and photographed, review the images on the camera with the students to see if they photographed the correct items.

4. Praise the students for identifying and photographing the items.

5. Print the photographs and present them to the students. Sort the items according to the different criteria used.

Evaluation

- Use the Evaluation Form (Teacher Version) (page 222) to record the students' progress.

- Fill out the Evaluation Form (Student Version) (page 223) with the student.

UPLOADING AND PRINTING (ADVANCED ACTIVITY)

Instructional format

Individual student or small group.

Learning objective

This activity will increase awareness of digital photography and its processes, including how the picture in the camera becomes the actual photograph.

Materials

Digital camera with at least five mega pixels and a removable memory card; computer with available USB ports; memory card reader or USB cables to import images from camera; photo printer; photo paper; a file for each student on the computer to store photos.

Procedure

1. Once students are finished taking photographs, direct them to the computer and show them the process of uploading the photographs.

2. Explain to the students that the purpose of uploading the pictures from the camera to the computer is to save the pictures on the computer to print later, and to make room on the camera for more pictures.

3. If using a USB cable, plug the cable into the digital camera and connect it to the computer. If using a memory card reader, remove the memory card from the camera and insert the card into the card reader. Open the folder containing the pictures.

4. Drag the images from the camera to the student's file folder.

5. Eject the memory card from the computer and insert it back into the camera.

6. Go back into the student's file folder on the computer and print the photographs.

7. Provide the students with their photographs and praise them.

PHOTOGRAPHY AND COLORING (ADVANCED ACTIVITY)

Instructional format

Individual student or small group.

Learning objective

In this activity, participants use both their existing photography skills and color pencils to create one-of-a-kind pictures.

Materials

Digital camera with at least five mega pixels with optical zoom capability and a removable memory card; computer with available USB ports; memory card reader or USB cables to import images from camera; photo printer, heavyweight multipurpose art paper (can be found in a painting sketchbook); a file for each student on the computer to store photos; colored pencils.

Procedure

1. Take the students to an outdoor location where they can photograph houses, plant life, other people's faces, or landscapes.

2. Let each student take several photographs and prompt them to photograph several different items. Encourage them to photograph some light colored objects so that the black and white photographs can be colored for the second part of this activity.

3. If they are photographing houses, instruct them to focus on one part of the house (window, door, etc.). If they are photographing flowers or plants, instruct them to get very close, about one foot away. If they are photographing someone's face, they should be two feet away. For landscapes, distance does not matter.

4. Return to the computer and download each student's photos, saving them in their folders.

5. Have the students choose two or three photographs.

6. Have the students convert their photographs to black and white (either in the camera or in the computer) and print them onto heavyweight multipurpose art paper.

7. Have the students color their photographs; prompt them to choose at least three colors.

8. Prompt the students to find shapes and color the shapes.

9. Praise the students and let them decide where to display their works of art. In Figure 11.9 Johnny McKenna, a student, presents the photograph he took and then colored. Johnny is very talented in drawing and photography, and the My Own World project allowed him to share his talent with the community and be recognized for his talents. Johnny received a certificate of honor for his artistic work from Providence Mayor Cicillini. Johnny's mother nurtures and encourages Johnny to make this a career.

Figure 11.9 Johnny McKenna's photograph, and the colourized version (held by Johnny)

CONNECTION TO CURRENT EVENTS (BASIC ACTIVITY)

Example: rising water during a flood in the springtime.

Instructional format

Individual student or small group.

Learning objective

This activity will foster a sense of being part of the community. Participants will create a historical documentation of an event that affected their environment and those around them.

Materials

Digital camera; photo printer; photo paper.

Procedure

1. Discuss the current weather event with the students (when did the rain start, how many inches of rain fell, what parts of the area were most affected, when was the last time a flood occurred, etc.).

2. Ask each student to state ways the flood has personally affected them.

3. Take the students to view the rising water in the river.

4. Have students take turns taking photographs of the river.

5. Return to the computer, download and print the photos.

6. Let the students decide where to display their photos.

7. In Figure 11.10 we show two examples of current events photographed by students.

Figure 11.10 Photograph of President Obama, taken directly from the newspaper, and a photograph of a rising river

PHOTOGRAPHY-RELATED COMPUTER SKILLS (INTERMEDIATE ACTIVITY)

A task analysis format is used to teach photography-related computer skills to the students. Many students with autism require this kind of support to organize and sequence the steps needed to learn a new task or skill. Tables 11.2, 11.3, and 11.4 are examples that outline the task analysis used to teach photography-related computer skills (the steps may need to be modified depending on the computer and software being used, and the competence level of students using them).

Table 11.2 Basic computer operations

Task	Skill acquired (date)	Staff initials
Locate the computer workshop		
Identify computer to work on		
Turn on the computer		
Turn on the monitor (if necessary)		
Use the mouse		
Identify the different icons on the computer desktop		
Turn the computer and monitor off		

Table 11.3 Adding a photograph to a personal file

Task	Skill acquired (date)	Staff initials
Find or identify the photograph software program		
Open up the software program		
Open up personal file		
Add a picture by clicking on the icon		
Learn how to browse for the appropriate folder		
Click on the proper folder		
Locate the picture		
Click on the picture		
Click on the 'add picture' icon		
Click on the 'done' icon		
Close the software program		

Table 11.4 Editing a picture in photograph software program

Task	Skill acquired (date)	Staff initials
Double click on the picture		
Click on 'edit picture'		
Select correct editing feature (crop, etc.)		
Click on the chosen picture to highlight it		
Double click on the picture to open it to a full size image		
Click the 'edit' icon		
Use the selected editing feature on the picture (see Figure 11.11 for example)		
Click on 'accept'		
Save the picture with a new name (with teacher support)		
Close the software program		

Original photo

Edited photo example I

Edited photo example II

Figure 11.11 Editing a picture in photograph software program

Chapter 12

Measuring Positive Traits

The ASPeCT-DD Scale

This book is focused on a number of positive traits that can lead to a fuller and more enriched quality of life for persons with developmental disabilities. Not only can we help people to improve their own situation by decreasing non-desired behaviors, but also we can help by supporting and enhancing traits that make lives better or more enjoyable. But how would we know what positive traits to focus on? And how would we know if we had actually made a difference? These are difficult questions to answer, and so a number of years ago, we began working on a scale to measure positive traits in persons with developmental disabilities (Woodard 2006). If we could know how much of any given trait a person possessed, perhaps we could maximize the use of this trait. Or, if we knew that a particular trait was lacking, we could really focus our energies on helping that person to improve that trait.

There is other research on scales designed to measure the related concept of 'quality of life.' In research with persons with developmental disabilities (e.g., Sheppard-Jones *et al.* 2005), survey instruments tapped quality of life components by including relationships, safety, health, choice-making opportunities, community participation, well-being and satisfaction, and rights. The resulting measure, the Core Indicators Consumer Survey (Human Services Research Institute 2001), includes items identified as related to personal perception (and well-being). These specifically include items such as 'Are you ever afraid or scared when you are at home?' and 'Do you have a best friend?' which may indirectly tap internally based perceptions and traits such as courage, kindness, and empathy. But Dykens (2006) reports that only 1 percent of quality of life questions are related to happiness, contentment, or zest for life, as compared to 58 percent of the questions that dealt with specific external conditions. Further and perhaps most importantly, Dykens (2006) cites observations by Edgerton (1996) that suggest finding or creating happiness and contentment depends mainly on internal dispositions, characteristics, and thinking styles rather than simply taking stock of what is externally available. That is, quality of life may be less determined by what you have, and more determined by what you choose to do with what you have.

POSITIVE TRAITS AND WELL-BEING

So if there are character strengths, positive traits, or dispositional perceptions that contribute to quality of life, what exactly are they? As noted in this introduction, this is a question often asked by researchers of positive psychology (Seligman and Csikszentmihalyi 2000), which is a growing area of psychology with its roots in the works of psychologists such as Abraham Maslow and Carl Rogers. Researchers in this area have begun to explore some of these 'elusive' internal dispositions and characteristics that current quality of life research for persons with developmental disabilities have not as yet fully tapped. While not an exhaustive listing, Seligman (2002) suggests that they include hope, optimism, gratitude, and forgiveness, and researchers (Shogren et al. 2006) have also identified the important role of selected traits (e.g., optimism) in predicting life satisfaction. Others have suggested that unique concepts such as 'flow' may contribute to happiness (Nakamura and Csikszentmahalyi 2005), self-efficacy is needed for success (Maddux 2005), and humor is related to lessened depression and may moderate stress regardless of the intensity of the stressor (Lefcourt 2005). Still other researchers propose positive effects of courage, kindness, and resilience, yet rarely are such characteristics measured and targeted for improvement in persons with developmental disabilities (with the exception of empathy; e.g., Baron-Cohen and Wheelwright 2004). Omitting these areas from the assessment, training, treatment, or supports that a person with developmental disabilities receives may remove important variables affecting quality of life.

CHALLENGES IN EVALUATING POSITIVE TRAITS IN PERSONS WITH DEVELOPMENTAL DISABILITIES

There may be a variety of reasons why such traits or internal dispositions have not traditionally been measured in persons with developmental disabilities, either as elements of quality of life or the sub-category of well-being. Limited resources may have needed to be directed toward more pressing problem behavior reduction, although we would suggest that maximizing positive traits may prove to have the same effect. Other challenges may include the assessment procedure itself. Options for assessment have traditionally included interviews or questionnaires (Hughes *et al.* 1995), but such procedures often depend on the accurate and effective communication skills, cognitive capacities, and self-reflection, self-observation, and introspection abilities of the person being assessed, which are often areas of deficit for persons with developmental disabilities. Other options for assessment include direct observation or permanent product measures, which are externally oriented procedures familiar to the behaviorally trained researcher or practitioner. But these types of measures are not well suited to measuring the internal perceptions, traits, or dispositions that are the focus of this study. This is because the behavioral markers reflective of these internal positive traits or perceptions are likely to be subtly and infrequently expressed in highly individualistic, context specific ways, by persons for whom the expression of courage, for example, is very unique.

For these reasons, a fourth option was selected: an informant-report survey measure completed by staff who spent extended amounts of time with the person being evaluated. While this type of assessment capitalizes on the sensitivity, positivity, and intuitive skills often present in staff who work with persons with developmental disabilities, there are also distinct limitations and challenges. Informant-report survey measures may decrease the accuracy of the assessment not only because it is not the person being evaluated who is completing the survey, but also because the evaluator may introduce distinct biases. Researchers may introduce procedures to minimize these (e.g., specific instructions) or try to measure their impact (e.g., inter-rater reliability measures), but some error will certainly persist as a result of using this method. In the following study, we chose to accept the potential for error associated with this form of assessment, rather than not attempt to measure positive traits or create behavioral measures that may or may not reflect the strengths of interest.

CREATION OF A TOOL FOR MEASURING POSITIVE TRAITS: THE ASPECT STUDY

One hundred and sixty nine children and adults diagnosed with a developmental disability (autism, pervasive developmental disorder (PDD-NOS), Asperger's syndrome, or mental retardation) were assessed using the ASPeCT-DD (Assessment Scale for Positive Character Traits – Developmental Disabilities), as well as the positive and negative scales of the Nisonger Child Behaviour Rating Form (NCBRF; Aman 1991). We conducted a factor analysis on ASPeCT-DD scores, and explored test-retest reliability by comparing a portion of the sample's scores to scores collected nine months earlier. We also explored validity by correlating ASPeCT-DD scores with positive and negative scales of the NCBRF. We hypothesized that test-retest reliability would be high, and that ASPeCT-DD scores would show high correlations with the positive scales of the NCBRF, and low or negative correlations with the negative NCBRF scales.

ASPeCT-DD is a 26-item scale developed at the Groden Center, and is composed of items assessing ten positive trait areas: empathy, optimism, forgiveness, kindness, humor, gratitude, self-efficacy, courage, self-control, and resilience. Trait areas were selected and items were generated from a review of literature on positive psychology, and certain items were adapted from other scales including the Life Orientation Test-Revised (LOT-R; Carver and Scheier 2003); Child-Report Sympathy Scale (Zhou, Valiente and Eisenberg 2003); Heartland Forgiveness Scale (Thompson and Snyder 2003); The Empathy Quotient (Baron-Cohen and Wheelwright 2004); The Self-Efficacy Scale (Choi 2003); Gratitude, Resentment, and Appreciation Test (GRAT; Watkins et al. 2003); Self-Control Scale (Tangney, Baumeister and Boone 2004). The scale is completed by someone who is familiar with the person being rated, and he or she rates the person on a five-point Likert scale. Total scores can range from a low of 26 to a high of 130.

Additionally, ratings on the Nisonger Child Behaviour Rating Form (parent version) (NCBRF; Aman et al. 1996) were used. This is a 76-item informant-based questionnaire developed to assess two positive social areas (compliant/calm and adaptive social), and six behavior and emotional problem areas in children (conduct problems, insecure/anxious, hyperactive, self-injury, stereotypic, self-isolated/ritualistic, and overly sensitive). The NCBRF has been evaluated for reliability (e.g., Girouard, Morin and Tasse 1998), and validated with other measures (e.g., Aman et al. 1996).

WHAT WE FOUND

The average total score on the ASPeCT-DD for this group was 80.45, with a standard deviation of 13.32. The scores ranged from 40 to 121. Means and standard deviations for the individual factors are presented in Table 12.1.

Table 12.1 Means and standard deviations for individual factors

Factor	Mean	SD
Factor 1 (Positive Relations)	30.01	9.55
Factor 2 (Active Coping)	20.62	4.86
Factor 3 (Acceptance Coping)	15.28	4.08
Factor 4 (Positive Outlook)	14.45	3.09

Analysis of the data suggested either a three- or four-factor solution, and a four-factor solution was selected as no item loaded >0.40 on more than one factor. This four-factor solution is represented in Table 12.2.

Table 12.2 Factor structure of the Assessment Scale for Positive Character Traits – Developmental Disabilities (ASPeCT-DD)

(#) Items	Factor 1	Factor 2	Factor 3	Factor 4
(2) Empathy 1	0.71			
(6) Empathy 2	0.91			
(9) Empathy 3	0.89			
(13) Empathy 4	0.88			
(4) Kindness 1	0.82			
(8) Kindness 2	0.87			
(18) Gratitude 1	0.79			
(26) Self-efficacy 2	0.62			
(3) Humor 1	0.47			
(17) Humor 2	0.42			

(1) Courage 1	0.70		
(12) Courage 2	0.62		
(10) Resilience 1	0.74		
(14) Resilience 2	0.47		
(15) Self-control 2	0.52		
(21) Self-control 3	0.66		
(20) Self-efficacy 1	0.78		
(5) Forgiveness 1		0.66	
(7) Forgiveness 2		0.42	
(23) Forgiveness 3		0.55	
(24) Forgiveness 4		0.79	
(11) Self-control 1		0.79	
(16) Optimism 1			0.78
(25) Optimism 2			0.86
(19) General Happiness			0.57
(22) Gratitude 2			0.56

ASPeCT-DD total scores collected in October 2007 were compared to scores collected in January 2006; 61 of the 77 students for whom ASPeCT-DD scores were available in October 2007 also had scores recorded in January 2006. The correlation between these two sets of scores was fair ($r = 0.56$). Further, ASPeCT-DD scores for the entire sample ($n = 168$) were correlated with each of the two positive sub-categories and six negative sub-categories on the NCBRF to evaluate the validity of the scale. Total ASPeCT-DD scores were moderately correlated with the positive scales (Table 12.3), and not correlated to any notable degree to the sub-category scores for conduct problems, insecure/anxious, hyperactive, or overly sensitive. Interestingly, negative correlations were found for total ASPeCT-DD scores and the self-injury/stereotypic and self-isolated/ritualistic sub-category scores.

Table 12.3 Correlations of the Assessment Scale for Positive Character Traits –
Developmental Disabilities (ASPeCT-DD)

Scores with NCBRF Sub-category Scores		
NCBRF Sub-categories: Positive		**ASPeCT-DD**
1	Compliant/calm	0.56**
2	Adaptive/social	0.64**
NCBRF Sub-categories: Negative		
1	Conduct problems	-0.19*
2	Insecure/anxious	0.18*
3	Hyperactive	-0.15
4	Self-injury/stereotypic	-0.39**
5	Self-isolated/ritualistic	-0.39**
6	Overly sensitive	-0.09

*indicates significance at the $p < 0.05$ level
**indicates significance at the $p < 0.01$ level

WHAT IT ALL MEANS

The results of an examination of the psychometric properties of the
ASPeCT-DD demonstrates a strong factor structure: factor 1: traits
that serve to foster positive relations with others (Positive Relations);
factor 2: active engagement and coping with challenging problems
(Active Coping); factor 3: traits that promote positive coping through
acceptance (Acceptance Coping); and factor 4: happiness and positive
outlook on life (Positive Outlook). The first factor is clearly related to
social or interpersonal relationships and assesses the quality (not amount
or presence) of interactions. It asks whether or not they are marked by
empathy, kindness, and humor. Our second and third factors, active and
acceptance-based coping, support taking part in new, unfamiliar, or fearful
activities, 'bouncing back' or accepting and moving past failure, hurt, or
disappointment, and maintaining self-control under stress. Such positive
skill groupings might easily color or affect many of the quality of life
concepts. The fourth and final factor is the chosen perception of seeing

the bright side of life, and having a positive explanatory style. While quality of life measures may ask whether or not a person is happy, rarely do they ask if the person is actively trying to explain or understand events in his or her life in a way that creates this happiness! The four factors of the ASPeCT-DD are clearly related to the concepts of quality of life: the positive character trait groupings ask what internal traits are available and to what extent.

We chose to establish validity with the positive scales of the NCBRF not only because the scale was widely used, but also because the items included wording related to the internal trait perspective we were pursuing. For example, interactions with others were both 'positive' and 'initiated' by the person being rated. Not only were rules followed but also redirection was 'accepted,' and there were questions related to empathy and kindness ('Shared with or helped others'). Finally, there were questions related to self-control ('Resisted provocation, was tolerant') as well as the presentation of a happy or cheerful demeanor. Correlations with the two positive scales of the NCBRF were moderate as expected, so we went on to explore correlations with the NCBRF negative sub-category scores. What we expected and found was relatively low, at times negative correlations. It is notable that the two very negative correlations were found between ASPeCT-DD scores and the NCBRF sub-categories related to self-injury, isolation, and stereotypic and ritualistic behavior. This may suggest that as people with a developmental disability become more engaged with people and events in the world, they focus less on inwardly directed or self-based behavioral practices.

As positive psychology is an emerging field, research related to persons with developmental disabilities is limited. There are some examples of research designed to explore the effects of interventions on select positive traits in persons with developmental disability, and these studies both adapt interventions used with typically developing persons, and add new options. Agran et al. (2002) trained students with developmental disabilities to identify (verbally or with the aid of cue cards) problems and take personal responsibility for creating potential solutions. Reeve et al. (2007) used video modeling, directed prompting, and token reinforcement to increase helping behaviours that generalized to novel settings and stimuli. To further this exploratory effort, the present book begins to create activities for the purpose of equipping people with developmental disabilities with some of the internal, person-based strengths that may augment quality of life. The ASPeCT-DD is a first effort at assessing some of the positive traits of interest, so we can have some idea where best to direct resources. It is our hope that by increasing traits such as self-efficacy, empathy, kindness, courage, optimism, and resilience, we can maximize the active role persons with developmental disabilities can have in creating their own happiness and quality of life.

Chapter 13

Methods and Terms

This chapter describes methods and terms mentioned throughout the book. The purpose of this chapter is to assist parents and teachers in implementing the activities.

ANTECEDENTS

An antecedent is any event in the environment that occurs before a behavior. Antecedents help us to understand under what conditions a certain behavior is taking place.

CONSEQUENCES

Consequences are events or stimuli in the environment that occur after a behavioral response. The consequence of a behavior is an important component in the motivation of an individual to perform or desist from engaging in a behavior. Consequences that increase the probability of a behavior's recurrence are called reinforcers. Consequences that decrease a behavior's probability are termed punishers or extinction.

DISCRETE TRIAL INSTRUCTION

Discrete trial instruction (DTI) or discrete trial training is a highly structured teaching technique that typically involves a teacher working one-to-one with a student in a setting without distractions. Each trial has a definite or discrete beginning and end. DTI is based on the principles of Applied Behavior Analysis and has been used in teaching children with autism and other developmental disabilities since the 1970s. Ivar Lovaas' landmark research project with young children with autism (Lovaas 1987) demonstrated that intensive training (40 hours per week) using DTI as one of the primary teaching methods resulted in clinically significant improvement in academic and social areas for 47 percent of the students. The children who made such dramatic improvements were indistinguishable from their non-disabled peers by the time they were in first grade.

There are four main components to discrete trial instruction. They are:

1. *The instruction*: in descriptions of DTI you may see this referred to as the antecedent or more specifically the discriminative stimulus (SD) to which you want the child to respond. Depending on the type of DTI, the SD might be an environmental cue. When giving instructions in DTI, they should be clear and concise. Note: Sometimes, DTI also includes a prompting stimulus or cue from the teacher to help the child respond.

2. *The response*: this is the student's action elicited by the instruction. Prior to beginning instruction, the teacher must determine what the acceptable response(s) is (are) for the specific instruction. Responses are measured as correct, incorrect, or no response.

3. *The consequence*: this is what occurs immediately after the student's response. For a correct response, the consequence would be some sort of reinforcing stimulus. For an incorrect response, a correction procedure that has been planned in advance should be implemented. There are several ways to respond to an incorrect trial:

   ○ End the trial and begin a new one after a brief pause.

   ○ Show the student the correct response and repeat the trial.

   ○ Prompt the correct response using the next step in a prompt hierarchy.

4. *The inter-trial interval*: this refers to the brief pause between consecutive teaching trials in the DTI method.

ERRORLESS LEARNING

Errorless learning is an instructional strategy designed to produce correct and successful responses from the student, by preventing errors during the process of learning. Errorless learning is especially appropriate when teaching a new skill or asking for a novel response from a student who is challenged by frustration or is confused by a trial and error approach. Errorless learning provides the student with continuous prompting and modeling of the anticipated behavior, and reduces the chances of failure.

Following is an example of errorless learning, learning to write the letter H:

Errorless learning is best used with a within stimulus prompt so that a prompt is faded within the learning objective. In the above case the dots start close together and then fade to further apart.

Tips for implementing errorless learning

- Make sure that the skill being taught is appropriate for the student's current needs and level of ability.
- Use prompts that will ensure success.
- Select and use effective reinforcers and specific positive feedback.
- Always finish a session with a successful trial.

EXTINCTION

Extinction involves withholding reinforcement that had previously maintained a behavior in the past, resulting in the decrease in the rate of that behavior. An example of extinction is someone who stops receiving attention for whining, and the rate of whining decreases.

FUNCTIONAL ANALYSIS

Functional analysis is the identification of antecedents and consequences associated with the targeted behavior. The purpose of the behavior is assessed by looking at the conditions that maintain the behavior. This is accomplished by direct observation and recording data, which is then analyzed to produce patterns that help to identify the function of the behavior. Interventions are then designed based on information from the functional analysis.

MODELING

Modeling involves learning by observing another individual (a model) engage in behavior. The observer need not perform the behavior, nor receive direct consequences for his or her performance.

Video self-modeling (VSM) is an intervention where individuals learn skills by observing themselves performing the targeted skill appropriately via video. Voiceover can be included to emphasize relevant information. When children view the videotape, they see themselves as being able to perform the task in a successful manner.

PICTURE REHEARSAL

Picture rehearsal programs are a unique adaptation of imagery-based therapy, which combine a behavioral approach to learning with a visual support system. This results in an effective, internally mediated self-control strategy (Groden and LeVasseur 1995). This method is a proactive instructional strategy, based on sequenced pictures and an accompanying script. The pictures and script create a scene or story which describes when, where, and how to use a particular behavioral sequence, and ends with reinforcement for successful performance. The behavioral sequence depicted is typically a coping strategy, individually designed for use in situations that have been identified as stressful for the learner.

Picture rehearsal scenes are written within the positive reinforcement framework and have three components: the antecedent situation, the desired sequence of adaptive behavior, and the reinforcer for appropriate behavior. In response to the antecedent stressor, a coping strategy is added that targets self-control such as, 'I take a deep breath and relax' or, 'I know I can do it.' Each scene is designed to match the individual's attention abilities, language level, sequencing abilities, and picture preferences. Daily practice of the picture rehearsal scene increases the likelihood that the individual will be able to use it when the actual situation occurs. Note that maladaptive behavior is not mentioned in the script, as the focus of the daily practice is to help the individual imagine and internalize only the adaptive coping strategy and behavior. The following is an example of picture rehearsal text and the function of each part:

- *Antecedent*: 'I'm getting my tray in the cafeteria line. I put my hand in my pocket to get my lunch ticket. The ticket is not there.'

- *Coping strategy*: 'I take a slow deep breath and say to myself, relax. I count to five slowly and take another deep breath. I stay calm and tell myself, I can solve this problem.'

- *Behavior*: 'I look in my other pockets and find the ticket.'

- *Consequence (reinforcer)*: 'I feel better because I stayed calm and found the lunch ticket. Now I imagine myself getting a high five from my teacher for staying calm!'

For each individual, creation of a picture rehearsal scene requires information that is collected and obtained from observation, functional analysis, and paper and pencil measure.

PRECURSORS

Behaviors that may signal that more severe behaviors are about to occur. An example of this would be a student pursing his or her lips and uttering high sounds. When the teacher recognizes that this behavior is usually followed by more severe behaviors, the teacher can intervene to stop an escalation from happening. Identifying antecedents and precursors is important because they allow teachers to intervene prior to a target behavior.

PROMPTING

Prompting students provides them with information about how to respond successfully to tasks or directions that are reasonably challenging, and thus increases the probability of a correct response. Successful prompting leads to successful task completion and reinforcing feedback. The student is more likely to give the same response independently the next time, resulting in an accumulation of successful experiences.

The most common instructional prompts are:

- *Physical*: physical prompts can range from a full prompt in which the student is physically led through the activity, to a slight touch or tap on the shoulder or hand.

- *Gestural*: rather than touching the student, a teacher may provide an exaggerated gesture (a large wave or emphatic point) or a subtle movement (shift in eye gaze or slight point) that instructs the student on what to do or where to focus.

- *Verbal*: verbal prompts can range from specific detailed directions, to a truncated verbal cue (when prompting a verbal response), to general comments such as 'keep going.'

PUNISHMENT

Punishment is any consequence that is intended to decrease the future frequency of behavior that it follows. Punishment may have less desirable effects associated with it.

REINFORCEMENT

A consequence that maintains or increases the frequency of the behavior it follows. A reinforcer is defined only by the effect it has on the behavior.

Reinforcements for good behaviors can be tangible (toys or candy), activity based (going for a walk), or social (a smile or praise). Note that a reinforcer is a reinforcer only if the behavior it follows is strengthened, and what reinforces a student with autism may be quite different from what reinforces a typically developing person's behavior. The teacher needs to determine the reinforcers keeping in mind that reinforcers should be rotated to avoid satiation and be suitable for the environment.

The easiest way to identify reinforcers is by direct observation. There are also preference assessments where sets of potential reinforcers are presented in a planned manner. Also, paper and pencil reinforcement surveys (Cautela 1990) help caregivers provide information about their child's preferences. Generally this process will lead to the identification of several potential reinforcements that can then be tried to determine if they actually increase the goal behavior. Once several reinforcements are identified, it is important to begin pairing them with more naturally occurring reinforcements of a social nature. For example, praise is a natural, convenient, and socially valid reinforcement that could be used. However, praise may not be reinforcing to some individuals with autism. Nevertheless, by providing it simultaneously with the delivery of known reinforcements, it may gain reinforcing value with time.

A continuous reinforcement schedule provides reinforcement after every correct or desirable response. This type of schedule is useful when teaching a new response/skill. It emphasizes the relationship between the direction the teacher provides (discriminative stimulus) and the expected response which may result in quicker acquisition of the skill within the instructional setting. Continuous reinforcement schedules provide rich and predictable occurrences of rewards.

An intermittent reinforcement schedule dictates the provision of the reinforcement after performing the desired behavior every few times, or after a certain period of time.

RELAXATION

Youngsters with autism may frequently find themselves in a state of high stress, due to both the characteristics of the disorder itself (communication difficulties, poorly developed social skills, idiosyncratic sensory responses) and the lack of environmental accommodations. Helping them cope with stress requires not only reducing demands initially, but also developing coping processes that give persons with autism more control over their behavior. Relaxation is one of the most successful stress reduction strategies because it is a procedure that helps children gain self-control and cope more effectively with stress.

The progressive relaxation protocol described here was developed by Dr. Joseph Cautela and Dr. June Groden (Cautela and Groden 1978), and is tailored for children and adults with autism and other developmental disabilities. Stress produces both physiological and behavioral effects in an individual. Relaxation involves learning a set of responses that can be used to change a tense body state to a relaxed one, thereby reducing the stress being experienced. The individual first learns to discriminate between muscles that are tense and muscles that are relaxed. This is taught in a structured session, beginning with readiness skills if needed (sitting, eye contact and imitating), and moving to sequentially tightening and relaxing large muscle groups (arms, hands, legs). Physical prompts and modeling are often used during instruction, as well as immediate reinforcement for each successful trial. Breathing exercises are added next, and then a sequence of relaxing the muscle groups (without first tensing) is added. This routine is practiced daily. As individuals improve their ability to control muscle responses, other muscle groups are added to the routine, usually in a head to toe sequence. Relaxation prompts are provided by teachers or parents when signs of bodily tension are observed.

When the individual can respond reliably to relaxation prompts, instruction for when to use relaxation begins. The focus is on helping the individual identify both bodily signs of stress and the situations that elicit them. One advantage of relaxation therapy is that it can be used in any setting (school, home, or workplace), and whenever a stressful situation occurs. It is a positive, preventive strategy in which the learner actively reduces stress by engaging in a familiar routine that, through practice, can become inherently reinforcing.

Teaching relaxation to students with autism

It is best to teach the relaxation procedure when the student is alert and ready to learn. Find a quiet, comfortable place away from distractions. Have the student sit in a low chair so that his or her feet are touching the floor. Seat yourself in a low chair at eye level with the student. Use a schedule or picture to show the student what the activity is, and say, 'Time for relaxation.' For specific information, see *Relaxation: A Comprehensive Manual for Adults, Children, and Children with Special Needs* (Cautela and Groden 1978).

Strategies for practicing relaxation successfully

- It is important to go through the procedure slowly, making sure the student focuses on how good it feels to relax each body part.

- Many individuals with autism do not have good visual attention. However, it is important for the student to look at the teacher before asking the student to practice any skill. Gaining eye contact for even a brief period of time will usually get better results.

- Use specific verbal encouragement whenever possible. It is important to specify the behavior that is being praised. For example, say, 'That's good, you relaxed your _____' or, 'I like how you took that deep breath.'

- Spend more time relaxing than tightening (see Figure 13.1). Children are only learning how to make their muscles tight so they can feel the difference between tension and relaxation. After they learn to discriminate between tight muscles and relaxed muscles, drop the 'tighten' and have them just relax. It is important for generalization that children are able to relax without making their muscles tight first.

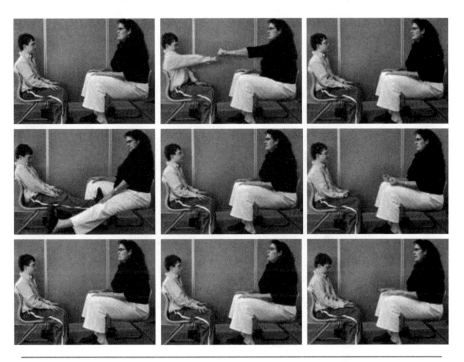

Figure 13.1 Students are taught to tighten and relax large muscle groups. Students learn to discriminate between tight muscles and relaxed muscles. Through repeated practice students eventually learn to relax in situations where they feel anxious. Relaxation provides pleasant physiological feedback. Students are more likely to perform better and interpret their performance in a positive way. This may foster confidence/self-efficacy

Using relaxation

Once students have learned the basics of the relaxation procedure and are able to respond to the cue 'relax,' they have a wonderful new skill in their behavioral repertoire. However, to reap the full benefits of the relaxation response, it is necessary to use relaxation in stressful situations. When the stressful situation occurs, the teacher prompts the student to 'relax.' After many trials using the teacher prompt, the goal is for the student to be able to identify the stressor and use relaxation as a self-control technique.

Identifying stressors

Through careful observation of physiological and behavioral events, a parent, teacher, or grandparent learns to recognize signs of stress. The student may begin talking too loudly, may wring his or her hands, start banging the table or show other signs that indicate distress. The Stress Survey Schedule for Individuals with Autism and Other Pervasive Developmental Disabilities (Groden *et al.* 2001) is a helpful tool to identify stressors. After making a list of the identified stressors, choose those stressors that are the most intense, most frequent, and those that prevent the student from participating in typical daily activities in the community.

ROLE-PLAYING

Role-plays are short rehearsals of desired behavioral sequences. Through role-playing, students can simulate a wide range of school, community, and workplace interactions. They can be tightly or loosely scripted depending upon the cognitive level of the student and the skill being taught. Often students are presented with a specific situation and asked to enact a particular scripted response as a behavioral rehearsal.

SELF-MANAGEMENT

Self-management is a procedure in which individuals change some aspect of their own behavior. One or more of four major components are generally involved: (1) self-selection of goals, (2) monitoring one's own behavior, (3) selection of procedures, and (4) implementation of procedures (Sulzer-Azaroff and Mayer 1991).

SETTING EVENTS

Setting events set the stage for behaviors that are likely to occur, and take into account the context, sometimes complex antecedent conditions, in which a behavior takes place. An example may be a student that becomes upset during a work session because it is taking place in a noisy environment. The noise in the environment is a contextual variable that has exerted some control over the stimulus–response relationship.

TASK ANALYSIS

Breaking down a complex skill or sequence of behaviors into small manageable consecutive steps, and teaching the steps separately (Sulzer-Azaroff and Mayer 1991). Task analysis provides a list of steps, or discrete behaviors, that are required to accomplish the task. An effective task analysis breaks down the skill into components, at a level of specificity that is dependent upon the learner. The following is an example of a task analysis for teaching tooth brushing:

1. Get toothbrush, glass, towel, and toothpaste.
2. Turn on cold water.
3. Wet toothbrush.
4. Fill glass with water.
5. Turn off water.
6. Remove cap from toothpaste.
7. Apply adequate amount of toothpaste to the brush.
8. Return cap to toothpaste.
9. Put toothpaste away.
10. Brush outside of teeth in front of mouth.
11. With upper and lower teeth meeting, brush outside of teeth in right side of mouth.
12. With upper and lower teeth meeting, brush outside of teeth in left of mouth.
13. Brush inside of lower right teeth.
14. Brush inside of lower left teeth.

15. Brush inside of upper right teeth.

16. Brush inside of upper left teeth.

17. Brush the biting surfaces of the teeth.

18. Turn on water.

19. Rinse toothbrush.

20. Turn off water.

21. Put toothbrush away.

22. Rinse mouth using glass of water.

23. Wash and dry face and hands using the towel.

24. Put towel away.

Writing a task analysis

There are a number of sources for task analyses, so check with these before you take the time to write one (see Lovaas 1981; Ford *et al.* 1996; Fredericks 1980a, 1980b). There are four essential components to writing a task analysis:

1. Identify the task to be taught.

2. Determine the essential components of the task.

3. Write the components in observable and understandable terms.

4. Arrange the components in sequential order.

Tips for refining and individualizing a task analysis

- Do the task yourself.
- Write down the steps.
- Have another person perform the task according to the written steps.
- Get feedback and correct the task analysis if needed.
- Do research – several published curricula provide task analyses for teaching a wide range of skills. These can be adapted for specific situations.
- Have the student perform the task according to the draft analysis.

- Adjust task analysis as needed by considering the size and sequence of the steps. The student may already know some steps; other steps may need to be broken down into smaller components.

- Accommodate or modify for individual needs such as cognitive or physical limitations.

How to teach using a task analysis

Shaping and chaining are commonly utilized methods associated with task analysis. *Shaping* is reinforcing the gradual and successive increases in the accuracy of the approximations made by the student, until he or she reaches the correct response. Shaping helps to build skills based upon what the student can do. *Chaining* involves linking each of the discrete behaviors in the program analysis together in a series, such that the result of each behavior is the stimulus (or antecedent) for the next. There are two commonly used methods of chaining: forward chaining and backward chaining.

In forward chaining the teacher introduces the first step. When the student grasps the first step, the second step becomes the focus of the teaching, and both steps are chained together. This continues until all steps are learned and the student can perform the task independently. For example, learning how to make a sandwich using forward chaining can start by learning to put two pieces of bread on the counter.

In backward chaining the first step taught is the last step in the task analysis. The remaining steps are gradually added from last to first until all steps are taught. Backward chaining is sometimes done if the last step is very reinforcing, such as watching a video. In this case the last step (pressing play button) may be the first step to be learned.

REFERENCES

Agran, M., Blanchard, C., Wehmeyer, M. and Hughes, C. (2002) 'Increasing the problem-solving skills of students with developmental disabilities participating in general education.' *Remedial and Special Education 23*, 5, 279–288.

Alderman, M.K. (2004) *Motivation for Achievement: Possibilities for Teaching and Learning.* Mahwah, NJ: Lawrence Erlbaum Associates.

Aman, M.G. (1991) *Assessing Psychopathology and Behavior Problems in Persons with Mental Retardation: A Review of Available Instruments.* Rockville, MD: U.S. Department of Health and Human Services.

Aman, M.G., Tasse, M.J., Rojahn, J. and Hammer, D. (1996) 'The Nisonger CBRF: A child behavior rating form for children with developmental disabilities.' *Research in Developmental Disabilities 17*, 41–57.

Ambron, S.R. and Irwin, D.M. (1975) 'Role taking and moral judgment in five- and seven-year-olds.' *Developmental Psychology 11*, 1, 102.

American Heritage Dictionary of the English Language (2006) *American Heritage Dictionary of the English Language*, 4th edition. Boston, MA: Houghton Mifflin.

Anderson, C.M. and Freeman, K.A. (2000) 'Positive behavior support: Expanding the application of applied behavior analysis.' *Behavior Analyst 23*, 1, 85–94.

Anderson, N.B. (ed.) (2000) Special Issue: *Positive Psychology. American Psychologist 55*, 1, 5–183.

Association for Applied and Therapeutic Humor (2005) Accessed on September 17, 2008 at www.aath.org.

Baer, D.M., Peterson, R.F. and Sherman, J.A. (1967) 'The development of imitation by reinforcing behavioral similarity to a model.' *Journal of the Experimental Analysis of Behavior 10*, 5, 405–416.

Bailey, D.B., Jr., Hatton, D.D., Mesibov, G., Ament, N. and Skinner, M. (2000) 'Early development, temperament, and functional impairment in autism and fragile X syndrome.' *Journal of Autism and Developmental Disorders 30*, 1, 49–59.

Bandura, A. (1993) 'Perceived self-efficacy in cognitive development and functioning.' *Educational Psychologist 28*, 117–148.

Bandura, A. (1997) *Self-Efficacy: The Exercise of Control.* New York: W.H. Freeman.

Barak, A., Engle, C., Katzir, L. and Fisher, W.A. (1987) 'Increasing the level of empathic understanding by means of a game.' *Simulation and Games 18*, 4, 458–470.

Barnett, M.A., Howard, J.A., Melton, E.M. and Dino, G.A. (1982) 'Effect of inducing sadness about self or other on helping behavior in high- and low-empathic children.' *Child Development 53*, 2, 920–923.

Barnhill, G.P. and Myles, B.S. (2001) 'Attributional style and depression in adolescents with Asperger syndrome.' *Journal of Positive Behavior Interventions 3*, 3, 175–182.

Baron, M.G., Lipsitt, L.P., Groden, J. and Groden, G. (2006) 'Introduction.' In M.G. Baron, J. Groden, G. Groden and L.P. Lipsitt (eds) *Stress and Coping in Autism.* New York: Oxford University Press.

Baron-Cohen, S. and Wheelwright, S. (2004) 'The empathy quotient: An investigation of adults with Asperger syndrome or high functioning autism, and normal sex differences.' *Journal of Autism and Developmental Disorders 34*, 2, 163–175.

Barrett, P.M., Sonderegger, R. and Xenos, S. (2003) 'Using friends to combat anxiety and adjustment problems among young migrants to Australia: A national trial.' *Clinical Child Psychology and Psychiatry 8*, 2, 241–260.

Batmanghelidjh, C. (1999) 'Whose political correction? The challenge of therapeutic work with inner-city children experiencing deprivation.' *Psychodynamic Counselling 5*, 2, 231–244.

Bauman, S.S.M. (ed.) (2002) *Fostering Resilience in Children.* Thousand Oaks, CA: Sage.

Bauminger, N., Shulman, C. and Agam, G. (2004) 'The link between perceptions of self and of social relationships in high-functioning children with autism.' *Journal of Developmental and Physical Disabilities 16*, 2, 193–214.

Bellini, S. (2004) 'Social skill deficits and anxiety in high-functioning adolescents with autism spectrum disorders.' *Focus on Autism and Other Developmental Disabilities 19*, 2, 78–86.

Bellini, S. and Akullian, J. (2007) 'A meta-analysis of video modeling and video self-modeling interventions for children and adolescents with autism spectrum disorders.' *Council for Exceptional Children 73*, 3, 264–287.

Bernard, M.E. (2004) 'Emotional resilience in children: Implications for rational emotive education.' *Journal of Cognitive and Behavioral Psychotherapies 4*, 1, 39–52.

Besser, A., Flett, G.L. and Hewitt, P. (2004) 'Perfectionism, cognition, and affect in response to performance failure vs. success.' *Journal of Rational-Emotive and Cognitive-Behavior Therapy 22*, 4, 301–328.

Betz, N.E. and Hackett, G. (1983) 'The relationship of mathematics self-efficacy expectations to the selection of science-based college majors.' *Journal of Vocational Psychology 23*, 3, 329–345.

Black, H. and Phillips, S. (1982) 'An intervention program for the development of empathy in student teachers.' *Journal of Psychology 112*, 159–168.

Blackshaw, A.J., Kinderman, P., Hare, D.J. and Chris, H. (2001) 'Theory of mind, causal attribution and paranoia in Asperger syndrome.' *Autism 5*, 2, 147–163.

Bouma, R. and Schweitzer, R. (1990) 'The impact of chronic childhood illness on family stress: A comparison between autism and cystic fibrosis.' *Journal of Clinical Psychology 46*, 6, 722–730.

Bracke, P., Christiaens, W. and Verhaeghe, M. (2008) 'Self-esteem, self-efficacy, and the balance of peer support among persons with chronic mental health problems.' *Journal of Applied Social Psychology 38*, 2, 436–459.

Branch, L.E. and Lichtenberg, J.W. (1987) *Self-Efficacy and Career Choice*. Education Resources Information Center. Accessed on October 10, 2008 at www.eric.ed.gov/ERICWebPortal/recordDetail?accno=ED289106.

Brissette, I., Scheier, M.F. and Carver, C.S. (2002) 'The role of optimism in social network development, coping, and psychological adjustment during a life transition.' *Journal of Personality and Social Psychology 82*, 1, 102–111.

Brooks, R.B. (ed.) (1999) *Fostering Resilience in Exceptional Children: The Search for Islands of Competence*. Dordrecht: Kluwer Academic.

Brooks, R.B. and Goldstein, S. (2001) *Raising Resilient Children*. New York: McGraw-Hill.

Brown, F., Belz, P., Corsi, L. and Wenig, B. (1993) 'Choice diversity for people with severe disabilities.' *Education and Training in Mental Retardation 28*, 4, 318–326.

Butzer, B. and Konstantareas, M.M. (2003) 'Depression, temperament and their relationship to other characteristics in children with Asperger's disorder.' *Journal on Developmental Disabilities 10*, 1, 67–72.

Carden Smith, L.K. and Fowler, S.A. (1984) 'Positive peer pressure: The effects of peer monitoring on children's disruptive behaviors.' *Journal of Applied Behavior Analysis 17*, 2, 213–227.

Carver, C.S. (no date) *Health Behavior Constructs: Theory, Measurement, and Research*. Accessed on October 6, 2008 at www.cancercontrol.cancer.gov/brp/constructs/dispositional_optimism/do5.html.

Carver, C.S. and Gaines, J.G. (1987) 'Optimism, pessimism, and postpartum depression.' *Cognitive Therapy and Research 11*, 449–462.

Carver, C.S. and Scheier, M. (2003) 'Optimism.' In S.J. Lopez and C.R. Snyder (eds) *Positive Psychological Assessment: A Handbook of Models and Measures*. Washington, DC: American Psychological Association.

Cautela, J. (1990) *Behavior Analysis Forms for Clinical Intervention, Vol. 2*. Beverly, MA: Cambridge Center for Behavioral Studies.

Cautela, J. and Groden, J. (1978) *Relaxation: A Comprehensive Manual for Adults, Children, and Children with Special Needs*. Champaign, IL: Research Press.

Charlop, M.H., Schreibman, L. and Tyron, A.S. (1983) 'Learning through observation: The effects of peer modeling on acquisition and generalization in autistic children.' *Journal of Abnormal Child Psychology 11*, 355–366.

Charlop-Christy, M.H. and Daneshvar, S. (2003) 'Using video modeling to teach perspective taking to children with autism.' *Journal of Positive Behavior Interventions 5*, 1, 12–21.

Choi, N. (2003) 'Further examination of the self-efficacy scale.' *Psychological Reports 92*, 473–480.

Clark, E., Olympia, D.E., Jensen, J., Heathfield, L.T. and Jenson, W.R. (2004) 'Striving for autonomy in a contingency-governed world: Another challenge for individuals with developmental disabilities.' *Psychology in the Schools 41*, 1, 143–153.

Clarke, P. (1984) 'What kind of discipline is most likely to lead to empathic behaviour in classrooms?' *History and Social Science Teacher 19*, 4, 240–241.

Costello, E.J. and Angold, A. (eds) (1995) *Epidemiology*. New York: Guilford Press.

Cotton, K. (2001) *Developing Empathy in Children and Youth*. Northwest Regional Educational Laboratory 31. Accessed on May 6, 2011 at http://educationnorthwest.org/webfm_send/556.

Creed, P.A., Patton, W.A. and Bartrum, D. (2004) 'Internal and external barriers, cognitive style, and the career development variables of focus and indecision.' *Journal of Career Development 30*, 4, 277–294.

Cunningham, E.G., Brandon, C.M. and Frydenberg, E. (2002) 'Enhancing coping resources in early adolescence through a school-based program teaching optimistic thinking skills.' *Anxiety, Stress and Coping 15*, 4, 369–381.

Dumas, J.E., Wolf, L.C., Fisman, S.N. and Culligan, A. (1991) 'Parenting stress, child behavior problems, and dysphoria in parents of children with autism, Down syndrome, behavior disorders, and normal development.' *Exceptionality 2*, 97–110.

Dweck, C.S. (2000) *Self Theories: Their Role in Motivation, Personality and Development*. Lillington, NC: Taylor & Francis.

Dyches, T.T., Cichella, E., Olsen, S.F. and Mandlesco, B. (2004) 'Snapshots of life: Perspectives of school-aged individuals with developmental disabilities.' *Research and Practice for Persons with Severe Disabilities 29*, 172–182.

Dykens, E.M. (2006) 'Toward a positive psychology of mental retardation.' *American Journal of Orthopsychiatry 76*, 185–193.

Edgerton, R.B. (1996) 'A Longitudinal-Ethnographic Research Perspective on Quality of Life.' In R.L. Schalock (ed.) *Quality of Life, Volume 1: Conceptualization and Measurement*. Washington, DC: American Association on Mental Retardation.

Eisenberg, N., Lennon, R. and Roth, K. (1983) 'Prosocial development: A longitudinal study.' *Developmental Psychology 19*, 6, 846–855.

Eisenberg-Berg, N. and Mussen, P. (1978) 'Empathy and moral development in adolescence.' *Developmental Psychology 14*, 2, 185–186.

Elicker, J., Englund, M. and Sroufe, L.A. (1992) 'Predicting Peer Competence and Peer Relationships in Childhood from Early Parent–Child Relationships.' In R.D. Parke and G.W. Ladd (eds) *Family–Peer Relationships: Modes of Linkage*. Hillsdale, NJ: Lawrence Erlbaum Associates.

Ellis, A. (1962) *Reason and Emotion in Psychotherapy*. New York: Lyle Stuart.

Emerich, D.M., Creaghead, N.A., Grether, S.M., Murray, D. and Grasha, C. (2003) 'The comprehension of humorous materials by adolescents with high-functioning autism and Asperger's syndrome.' *Journal of Autism and Developmental Disorders 33*, 3, 253–257.

Fall, M. and McLeod, E.H. (2001) 'Identifying and assisting children with low self-efficacy.' *Professional School Counseling 4*, 5, 334–341.

Fiedler, C.R. and Simpson, R.L. (1987) 'Modifying the attitudes of nonhandicapped high school students toward handicapped peers.' *Exceptional Children 53*, 4, 342–349.

Fisher, D., Pumpian, I. and Sax, C. (1998) 'High school students' attitudes about and recommendations for their peers with significant disabilities.' *Journal of the Association for Persons with Severe Handicaps 23*, 272–282.

Ford, A., Schnorr, R., Meyer, L., Davern, L., Black, J. and Dempsey, P. (1996) *The Syracuse Community-Referenced Curriculum Guide for Students with Moderate and Severe Disabilities*. Baltimore, MD: Paul H. Brooks Publishing Co.

Fowler, S.A. (1986) 'Peer-monitoring and self-monitoring: Alternatives to traditional teacher management.' Special Issue: *In Search of Excellence: Instruction that Works in Special Education Classrooms. Exceptional Children 52*, 6, 573–581.

Franzini, L.R. (2000) 'Humor in behavior therapy.' *Behavior Therapist 23*, 25–26, 28–29, 41.

Franzini, L.R. (2001) 'Humor in therapy: The case for training therapists in its uses and risks.' *Journal of General Psychology 128*, 2, 170–193.

Fredericks, H.D.B. (1980a) *The Teaching Research Curriculum for Moderately and Severely Handicapped. Gross and Fine Motor*. Prepared by the Teaching Research Infant and Child Center. Springfield, IL: Charles C. Thomas.

Fredericks, H.D.B. (1980b) *The Teaching Research Curriculum for Moderately and Severely Handicapped. Self-Help and Cognitive*. Prepared by the Teaching Research Infant and Child Center. Springfield, IL: Charles C. Thomas.

Frost, R.O., Marten, P.A., Lahart, C. and Rosenblate, R. (1990) 'The dimensions of perfectionism.' *Cognitive Therapy and Research 14*, 449–468.

Garber, J. and Flynn, C. (eds) (2001) *Vulnerability to Depression in Childhood and Adolescence*. New York: Guilford Press.

Gibran, K. (1997) *The Prophet*. Hertfordshire: Wordsworth Classics of World Literature.

Girouard, N., Morin, I. and Tasse, M. (1998) 'Étude de fidélité test-retest et accord interjuges de la Grille d'évaluation comportementale pour enfants Nisonger (GÉCEN).' *Revue Francophone de la Déficience Intellectuelle 9*, 2, 127–136.

Gladstone, T.R.G. and Kaslow, N.J. (1995) 'Depression and attributions in children and adolescents: A meta-analytic review.' *Journal of Abnormal Child Psychology 23*, 5, 597–606.

Goodwin, M., Groden., J., Velicer, W., Lipsitt, L.P., *et al.* (2006) 'Cardiovascular arousal in individuals with autism.' *Focus on Autism and Other Developmental Disabilities 21*, 2, 100–123.

Groden, G. (1989) 'A guide for conducting a comprehensive behavioral analysis of a target behavior.' *Journal of Behavior Therapy and Experimental Psychiatry 20*, 2, 163–169.

Groden, J., Baron, M.G. and Cautela, J. (1988) 'Behavioral Programming: Expanding our Clinical Repertoire.' In G. Groden and M.G. Baron (eds) *Autism: Strategies for Change.* New York: Gardner Press.

Groden, J. and Cautela, J. (1984) 'Use of imagery procedures with students labeled trainable retarded.' *Psychological Reports 54*, 2, 595–605.

Groden, J. and Cautela, J. (1988) 'Procedures to increase social interaction among adolescents with autism: A multiple baseline analysis.' *Behavior Therapy and Experimental Psychiatry 19*, 2, 87–93.

Groden, J., Cautela, J., Prince, S. and Berryman, J. (eds) (1994) *The Impact of Stress and Anxiety on Individuals with Autism and Developmental Disabilities.* New York: Plenum.

Groden, J., Diller, A., Bausman, M., Velicer, W., Norman, G. and Cautela, J. (2001) 'The development of a stress survey schedule for persons with autism and other developmental disabilities.' *Journal of Autism and Developmental Disorders 31*, 2, 207–217.

Groden, J. and LeVasseur, P. (1995) *Cognitive Picture Rehearsal: A System to Teach Self-Control.* Albany, NY: Delmar.

Groden, J., LeVasseur, P., Diller, A. and Cautela, J. (2002) *Coping with Stress through Picture Rehearsal: A How-To Manual for Working with Individuals with Autism and Developmental Disabilities.* Providence, RI: The Groden Center.

Herbek, T.A. and Yammarino, F.J. (1990) 'Empathy training for hospital staff nurses.' *Group and Organizational Studies 15*, 3, 279–295.

Hewitt, P. and Flett, G. (1991) 'Dimensions of perfectionism in unipolar depression.' *Journal of Abnormal Psychology 100*, 1, 98–101.

Higgins, D.J., Bailey, S.R. and Pearce, J.C. (2005) 'Factors associated with functioning style and coping strategies of families with a child with an autism spectrum disorder.' *Autism 9*, 2, 125–137.

Howard, J.A. and Barnett, M.A. (1981) 'Arousal of empathy and subsequent generosity in young children.' *Journal of Genetic Psychology 138*, 2, 307–308.

Hughes, C., Hwang, B., Kim, J., Eisenman, L. and Killian, D.J. (1995) 'Quality of life in applied research: A review and analysis of empirical measures.' *American Journal on Mental Retardation 99*, 6, 623–641.

Human Services Research Institute (2001) *Consumer Survey Phase II Technical Report.* Accessed on May 6, 2011 at www2.hsri.org/docs/PhaseII%20Consumer%20Survey%20Report-%20rei.pdf.

Kantor, A. and Groden, J. (2007) 'My own world.' *Autism and Related Developmental Disabilities 23*, 3, 1–4.

Kestenbaum, R., Farber, E.A. and Sroufe, L.A. (1989) 'Individual Differences in Empathy among Preschoolers: Relation to Attachment History.' In N. Eisenberg (ed.) *Empathy and Related Emotional Responses in New Directions for Child Development Series, Vol. 44.* San Francisco, CA: Jossey-Bass.

Keyes, C.L.M. and Lopez, S.J. (2002) 'Toward a Science of Mental Health: Positive Directions in Diagnosis and Interventions.' In C.R. Snyder and S.J. Lopez (eds) *Handbook of Positive Psychology.* New York: Oxford University Press.

Kim, J.A., Szatmari, P., Bryson, S.E., Streiner, D.L. and Wilson, F.J. (2000) 'The prevalence of anxiety and mood problems among children with autism and Asperger syndrome.' *Autism 4*, 2, 117–132.

Klauber, T. (1998) 'The significance of trauma in work with the parents of severely disturbed children, and its implications for work with parents in general.' *Journal of Child Psychotherapy 24*, 1, 85–107.

Krebs, D.L. and Russell, C. (1981) 'Role-Taking and Altruism.' In J.P. Rushton and R.M. Sorrentino (eds) *Altruism and Helping Behavior.* Hillsdale, NJ: Lawrence Erlbaum Associates.

Kremer, J.F. and Dietzen, L.L. (1991) 'Two approaches to teaching accurate empathy to undergraduates: Teacher-intensive and self-directed.' *Journal of College Student Development 32*, 69–75.

Kuiper, N.A. and Martin, R.A. (1998) 'Is Sense of Humor a Positive Personality Characteristic?' In W. Ruch (ed.) *The Sense of Humor: Explorations of a Personality Characteristic.* Humor Research Series, Vol. 3. Berlin: Mouton de Gruyter.

Ladd, G.W., Lange, G. and Stremmel, A. (1983) 'Personal and situational influences on children's helping behavior: Factors that mediate compliant helping.' *Child Development 54*, 2, 488–501.

Lazarus, R. (1991) *Emotion and Adaptation.* New York: Plenum.

Lee, S.-H., Simpson, R.L. and Shogren, K.A. (2007) 'Effects and implications of self-management for students with autism: A meta-analysis.' *Focus on Autism and Other Developmental Disabilities 22*, 1, 2–13.

Lefcourt, H.M. (2005) 'Humor.' In C.R. Snyder and S.J. Lopez (eds) *Handbook of Positive Psychology.* Oxford: Oxford University Press.

Lefcourt, H.M. and Thomas, S. (1998) 'Humor and Stress Revisited.' In W. Ruch (ed.) *The Sense of Humor: Explorations of a Personality Characteristic.* Humor Research Series, Vol. 3. Berlin: Mouton de Gruyter.

Lewis, J. (1999) 'Research into the concept of resilience as a basis for the curriculum for children with EBD.' *Emotional and Behavioural Difficulties 4*, 2, 11–22.

Linley, P.A. and Joseph, S. (eds) (2004) *Positive Psychology in Practice.* Hoboken, NJ: Wiley.

Loizou, E. (2006) 'Young children's explanation of pictorial humor.' *Early Childhood Education Journal 33*, 6, 425–431.

Lovaas, O.I. (1987) 'Behavioral treatment and normal educational and intellectual functioning in young autistic children.' *Journal of Clinical and Consulting Psychology 55*, 3–9.

Luszczynska, A. and Gutierrez-Donna, B. (2005) 'General self-efficacy in various domains of human functioning: Evidence from five countries.' *International Journal of Psychology 40*, 2, 80–89.

Lyubomirsky, S. and Lepper, H. (1999) 'A measure of subjective happiness: Preliminary reliability and construct validation.' *Social Indicators Research 46*, 137–166.

McCollough, T.E. (1992) *Trust and Ethics in School Reform*. Education Resources Information Center. Accessed on May 6, 2011 at www.eric.ed.gov/PDFS/ED353185.pdf.

McGhee, P.E. (1976) 'Children's appreciation of humor: A test of the cognitive congruency principle.' *Child Development 47*, 420–426.

McGhee, P.E. (1984) 'Play, Incongruity and Humor.' In T.K. Yawkey and A.D. Pellegrini (eds) *Child's Play: Developmental and Applied*. Mahwah, NJ: Lawrence Erlbaum Associates.

McGhee, P.E. (2003) *The Development of Young Children's Humor*. The Laughter Remedy Newsletter. Accessed on September 1, 2009 at www.humor.ch/mcghee/mcghee_03_01.htm.

Maddux, J.E. (2005) 'Self-Efficacy: The Power of Believing You Can.' In C.R. Snyder and S.J. Lopez (eds) *Handbook of Positive Psychology*. Oxford: Oxford University Press.

Maslow, A. (1971) *The Farther Reaches of Human Nature*. New York: Viking.

Masten, A.S. (2001) 'Ordinary magic: Resilience processes in development.' *American Psychologist 56*, 3, 227–238.

Masten, A.S., Best, K.M. and Garmezy, N. (1990) 'Resilience and development: Contributions from the study of children who overcome adversity.' *Development and Psychopathology 2*, 4, 425–444.

Masten, A.S. and Coatsworth, J.D. (1998) 'The development of competence in favorable and unfavorable environments: Lessons from research on successful children.' *American Psychologist 53*, 2, 205–220.

Masten, A.S. and Reed, M.G.J. (eds) (2002) *Resilience in Development*. New York: Oxford University Press.

Meyer, J.A., Mundy, P.C., Van Hecke, A.V. and Durocher, J.S. (2006) 'Social attribution process and comorbid psychiatric symptoms in children with Asperger syndrome.' *Autism 10*, 4, 383–402.

Morgan, S.R. (1983) 'Development of empathy in emotionally disturbed children.' *Humanistic Education and Development 22*, 2, 70–79.

Morrison, L., Kamp, D., Garcia, J. and Parker, D. (2001) 'Peer mediation and monitoring strategies to improve initiations and social skills for students with autism.' *Journal of Positive Behavior Interventions 3*, 237–250.

Muris, P., Steerneman, P., Merckelbach, H., Holdrinet, I. and Meesters, C. (1998) 'Comorbid anxiety symptoms in children with pervasive developmental disorders.' *Journal of Anxiety Disorders 12*, 4, 387–393.

Nakamura, J. and Csikszentmahalyi, M. (2005) 'The Concept of Flow.' In C.R. Snyder and S.J. Lopez (eds) *Handbook of Positive Psychology*. Oxford: Oxford University Press.

Nes, L.S. and Segerstrom, S.C. (2006) 'Dispositional optimism and coping: A meta-analytic review.' *Personality and Social Psychology Review 10*, 235–251.

Nettles, S.M., Mucherah, W. and Jones, D.S. (2000) 'Understanding resilience: The role of social resources.' *Journal of Education for Students Placed at Risk 5*, 1–2, 47–60.

Newman, B., Reinecke, D. and Meinberg, D. (2000) 'Self-management of varied responding in three students with autism.' *Behavioral Interventions 15*, 145–151.

Nilsen, A.P. and Nilsen, D.L.F. (1987) 'Parenting creative children: The role and evolution of humor.' *Creative Child and Adult Quarterly 12*, 1, 53–61.

Nilsen, A.P. and Nilsen, D.L.F. (1999) 'The straw man meets his match: Six arguments for studying humor in English classes.' *English Journal 88*, 34–42.

Nirje, B. (1969) 'The Normalization Principle and its Human Management Implications.' In R. Kugel and W. Wolfensberger (eds) *Changing Patterns in Residential Services for the Mentally Retarded*. Washington, DC: President's Committee on Mental Retardation.

Otake, K., Shimai, S., Tanaka-Matsumi, J., Otsui, K. and Fredrickson, B.L. (2006) 'Happy people become happier through kindness: A counting kindnesses intervention.' *Journal of Happiness Studies 7*, 361–375.

Pajares, F. (2002) *Overview of Social Cognitive Theory and of Self-Efficacy*. Accessed on October 3, 2010 at www.emory.edu/EDUCATION/mfp/eff.html.

Pajares, F. and Kranzler, J. (1995) 'Self-efficacy beliefs and general mental ability in mathematical problem-solving.' *Contemporary Educational Psychology 20*, 426–443.

Pecukonis, E.V. (1990) 'A cognitive/affective empathy training program as a function of ego development in aggressive adolescent females.' *Adolescence 25*, 97, 59–76.

Perry, D.G., Bussey, K. and Freiberg, K. (1981) 'Impact of adults' appeals for sharing on the development of altruistic dispositions in children.' *Journal of Experimental Child Psychology 32*, 127–138.

Peterson, C. and Seligman, M.E.P. (2004) *Character Strengths and Virtues: A Handbook and Classification*. Oxford: Oxford University Press.

Piper, W. (1930) *The Little Engine That Could*. New York: Matt and Plunk.

Prerost, F.J. (1988) 'Use of humor and guided imagery in therapy to alleviate stress.' *Journal of Mental Health Counseling 10*, 1, 16–22.

Prerost, F.J. (1989) 'Humor as an intervention strategy during psychological treatment: Imagery and incongruity.' *Psychology: A Journal of Human Behavior 26*, 4, 35–40.

Reeve, S.A., Reeve, K.F., Townsend, D.B. and Poulson, C.L. (2007) 'Establishing a generalized repertoire of helping behaviour in children with autism.' *Journal of Applied Behaviour Analysis 40*, 123–136.

Reis, S.M. and Colbert, R. (2004) 'Counseling needs of academically talented students with learning disabilities.' *Professional School Counseling 8*, 2, 156–167.

Reivich, K.J, Gillham, J.E., Chaplin, T.M. and Seligman, M.E.P. (2005) 'From Helplessness to Optimism.' In S. Goldstein and R.B. Brooks (eds) *Handbook of Resilience in Children.* New York: Kluwer Academic/Plenum.

Rogers, C. (1951) *Client-Centered Therapy.* Boston, MA: Houghton Mifflin.

Romanczyk, R.G. and Gillis, J.M. (2006) 'Autism and the Physiology of Stress and Anxiety.' In M.G. Baron, J. Groden, G. Groden and L.P. Lipsitt (eds) *Stress and Coping in Autism.* New York: Oxford University Press.

Ross, W.D. (ed.) (2010) *Rhetoric by Aristotle.* New York: Cosimo Classics.

Schacht, S. and Stewart, B.J. (1990) 'What's funny about statistics? A technique for reducing student anxiety.' *Teaching Sociology 18*, 1, 52–56.

Scholz, B.G., Dona, S.S. and Schwarzer, R. (2002) 'Is general self-efficacy a universal construct? Psychometric findings from 25 countries.' *European Journal of Psychological Assessment 18*, 242–251.

Schunk, D.H. (1985) 'Participation in goal setting: Effects on self-efficacy and skills of learning-disabled children.' *Journal of Special Education 19*, 3, 307–317.

Schunk, D.H. and Zimmerman, B.J. (2007) 'Influencing children's self-efficacy and self-regulation of reading and writing through modeling.' *Reading and Writing Quarterly 23*, 7–25.

Segal, J. (1988) 'Teachers have enormous power in affecting a child's self-esteem.' *Brown University Child Behavior and Development Newsletter 4*, 1–3.

Segerstrom, S.C. (2005) 'Optimism and immunity: Do positive thoughts always lead to positive effects?' *Brain, Behavior, and Immunity 19*, 3, 195–200.

Seligman, M.E.P. (2002) *Authentic Happiness.* New York: Free Press.

Seligman, M.E.P. and Csikszentmihalyi, M. (2000) 'Positive psychology: An introduction.' *American Psychologist 55*, 1, 5–14.

Seligman, M.E.P., Reivich, K., Jaycox, L. and Gillham, J. (1995) *The Optimistic Child: A Proven Program to Safeguard Children from Depression and Build Lifelong Resilience.* Boston, MA: Houghton Mifflin.

Seligman, M.E.P., Steen, T.A., Park, N. and Peterson, C. (2005) 'Positive psychology progress: Empirical validation of interventions.' *American Psychologist 60*, 5, 410–421.

Selman, R.L. (1971) 'Taking another's perspective: Role-taking development in early childhood.' *Child Development 42*, 6, 1721–1734.

Selman, R.L. (1975) 'Level of social perspective taking and the development of empathy in children: Speculations from a social-cognitive viewpoint.' *Journal of Moral Education 5*, 1, 35–43.

Selman, R.L. (1980) *The Growth of Interpersonal Understanding: Developmental and Clinical Analysis.* New York: Academic Press.

Sheppard-Jones, K., Prout, H.T. and Kleinert, H. (2005) 'Quality of life dimensions for adults with developmental disabilities: A comparative study.' *Mental Retardation 43*, 4, 281–291.

Shogren, K.A., Lopez, S.J., Wehmeyer, M.L., Little, T.D. and Pressgrove, C.L. (2006) 'The role of positive psychology constructs in predicting life satisfaction in adolescents with and without cognitive disabilities: An explanatory study.' *Journal of Positive Psychology 1*, 1, 37–52.

Snyder, C.R. (2002) 'Hope theory: Rainbows in the mind.' *Psychological Inquiry 13*, 4, 249–275.

Snyder, C.R. and Lopez, S.J. (eds) (2002) *Handbook of Positive Psychology.* New York: Oxford University Press.

Stahmer, A.C. and Schreibman, L. (1992) 'Teaching children with autism appropriate play in unsupervised environments using a self-management treatment package.' *Journal of Applied Behavior Analysis 25*, 2, 447–459.

Sulzer-Azaroff, B. and Mayer, G.R. (1991) *Behavior Analysis for Lasting Change.* Fort Worth, TX: Harcourt Brace College.

Tangney, J.P., Baumeister, R.F. and Boone, A.L. (2004) 'High self-control predicts good adjustment, less pathology, better grades, and interpersonal success.' *Journal of Personality 72*, 2, 271–324.

Thompson, L.Y. and Snyder, C.R. (2003) 'Measuring Forgiveness.' In S.J. Lopez and C.R. Snyder (eds) *Positive Psychological Assessment: A Handbook of Models and Measures.* Washington, DC: American Psychological Association.

Underwood, B. and Moore, B. (1982) 'Perspective-taking and altruism.' *Psychological Bulletin 91*, 1, 143–173.

Watkins, P.C., Woodward, K., Stone, T. and Kolts, R.L. (2003) 'Gratitude and happiness: Development of a measure of gratitude, and relationships with subjective well-being.' *Social Behavior and Personality 31*, 5, 431–451.

Werner, E.E. (2000) 'Protective Factors and Individual Resilience.' In J.P. Shonkoff and S.J. Meisels (eds) *Handbook of Early Childhood Intervention*, 2nd edition. New York: Cambridge University Press.

Wolfensberger, W. (1972) *Normalization: The Principle of Normalization in Human Services.* Toronto: National Institute on Mental Retardation.

Woodard, C.R. (2006) 'Psychometric properties of the ASPeCT-DD: Measuring positive traits in persons with developmental disabilities.' *Journal of Applied Research in Intellectual Disabilities 22*, 5, 433–444.

Yates, T.M. and Masten, A.S. (eds) (2004) *Fostering the Future: Resilience Theory and the Practice of Positive Psychology.* Hoboken, NJ: Wiley.

Zahn-Waxler, C., Radke-Yarrow, M. and King, R. (1979) 'Child rearing and children's prosocial initiations toward victims of distress.' *Child Development 50,* 319–330.

Zhou, Q., Valiente, C. and Eisenberg, N. (2003) 'Empathy and its Measurement.' In S.J. Lopez and C.R. Snyder (eds) *Positive Psychological Assessment: A Handbook of Models and Measures.* Washington, DC: American Psychological Association.

Zillman, D. (1977) 'Humour and Communication: An Introduction.' In A.J. Chapman and H.C. Foot (eds) *It's a Funny Thing, Humor.* Oxford: Pergamon.

SUBJECT INDEX

AUTHOR INDEX